"One Size Fits All"
and Other Fables

This is a book for women of all sizes. Liz poignantly shares her life journey as a large woman, helping all of us understand that our bodies are a gift — something to nurture and cherish for a lifetime.

Billie Gibson Hall
Director, Jane C. Stormont Women's
Health Center, Topeka, KS

Liz speaks from the heart — sharing insightful and thought-provoking issues related to size and self-concept. This empowering and loving text can be pivotal and life-changing for many who struggle with self-acceptance.

Michelle Kuntz Wood
Coordinator, Women's Health Services
St. Francis Hospital, Beech Grove, IN

"One Size Fits All"

and Other Fables

Liz Curtis Higgs

THOMAS NELSON PUBLISHERS
Nashville

Dedication

To my husband, Bill Higgs,
who waited almost thirty-four years
to marry this "big, beautiful woman ..."
your love makes everything possible.

June 1993

Published in Nashville, Tennessee, by Thomas Nelson, Inc.,
Publishers, and distributed in Canada by Word Communications,
Ltd., Richmond, British Columbia, and in the United Kingdom by
Word (UK), Ltd., Milton Keynes, England.

Scripture quotations are from the NEW KING JAMES VERSION of
the Bible. Copyright © 1979, 1980, 1982, Thomas Nelson, Inc.,
Publishers.

Library of Congress Cataloging-in-Publication Data

Higgs, Liz Curtis.
    "One size fits all" and other fables / Liz Curtis Higgs.
        p.   cm.
    Includes bibliographical references.
    ISBN 0-8407-6333-6
    1. Overweight women — Mental health.   2. Self-esteem in women.
3. Obesity — Psychological aspects.   4. Body image.   I.   Title.
RC552.O25H54   1993
158'.1'082 — dc20   93-20672
                                                                  CIP

Printed in the United States of America
1 2 3 4 5 6 7 - 99 98 97 96 95 94 93

Acknowledgments

Heartfelt thanks and many hugs to the hundreds of people who made these pages possible:

To the women whose comments appear here . . . thank you for your time, your courage and your honesty.

To: Catherine from Kentucky, Etta from Wisconsin, Melissa from New Jersey, Carla from New Hampshire, Fanny from Tennessee, Cindy from Illinois, Shirley from Arizona, Jan from Indiana, Bonita from Colorado, Mary from Pennsylvania, and Linda from Pennsylvania, who provided the names of each chapter, or "fable." Thank you for your creativity.

To the eleven remarkable women who shared their professional expertise through lengthy telephone interviews: Lynette, Anne, Robin, Kayla, Pat, Kathy, Nancye, Carole, Jeanne, Carol and Alice. Many thanks for sharing your time and talents.

To my friend and encourager, Duncan Jaenicke, with the terrible handwriting and wonderful insights. Thank you for believing in me.

To my National Coordinator, Pam Dennison, who kept our office humming. Thank you for sharing your many gifts (especially, patience!).

To Anne Dorton, who entered into my word processor — without a single typo! — the written responses of more than 200 wonderful women. Thank you for your commitment to getting it right.

To my friends and associates in the National Association of Women's Health Professionals. Thank you for your generous encouragement.

To Sonya Davis, who cared for our little ones, and kept them out of the study so I could press on. Thank you for being Mom #2.

To all my new friends at Thomas Nelson Books. You are simply the best.

To Bob Russell, who was the first to teach me about God's grace. I am ever in your debt.

To my father, D. Curtis Amidon, who always told me I was beautiful. You are, too, Daddy.

To my children, Matthew and Lillian, who make every morning Christmas. Thank you for letting me be your "Mama."

To you, who were kind enough to purchase this book. May it fill your heart!

Contents

Introduction

Back in October 1962, the Four Seasons had a #1 hit record, "Big Girls Don't Cry." Don't you believe it! More tears have been shed over expanding waistlines than all of life's other challenges combined, including departing sweethearts and declining bank accounts.

Each day brings a new diet book, and magazine racks shout monthly, "Lose 20 Pounds in 20 Days!" We buy it, we try it, we cry when it doesn't work. Everyone is dieting, but the only thing we're losing is our self-esteem.

For almost thirty years, my own self-esteem hovered somewhere between poor and pitiful (in the South, that's pronounced "p-i-i-i-tiful!"). Surrounded by my tiny cheerleader friends in school, I always felt fat, even though I was only a few pounds above the norm.

My first diet was at age ten, to be followed by dozens more in the years that followed. I was the classic yo-yo dieter: up and down, up and down.

Like many young women with low self-esteem, I didn't date much, and settled for any guy in pants when I did go out. I dropped out of college and landed in lots of dead-end jobs and going-nowhere relationships.

Call me the Prodigal Daughter. I had to try everything, had to hit rock bottom before I woke up.

That "wake up call" came soon after my thirtieth birthday. Weary of looking for love in all the wrong places, and trying to diet my way into some man's arms, I threw out every scale in the house (both the big kind you stand on and the little ones that weigh food) and announced to the world, "This is the Liz-that-is!"

A funny thing happened. The mountains didn't crumble and the earth didn't stop spinning. Over the next seven years, I bought the wardrobe I needed and deserved (instead of waiting until I was thin enough to "earn" it), married a wonderful man, started my own business, gave birth to two adorable children, bought my dream house in the country and started writing this book.

I am grateful for every blessing from above, but most of all for God's complete and loving acceptance of me, big hips and all. That's what helped me accept myself. That's what made the difference.

There are, at this moment, thousands of women across America who are still trying to diet their way to happiness. Not just big women, mind you, but medium size and thin women! We tell ourselves that if we "just lose 10 pounds" (or 20, 40, 60 or 100 pounds), we will look better, feel better, even be better people.

So much for complete and loving self-acceptance.

I believe that basing our self-worth on what the scale says means programming ourselves for disaster.

Such a heartless and fickle device, that bathroom scale! If we lose a quarter of a pound, we dance all the way to the doughnut store to celebrate. All this for a quarter of a pound. Four liquid ounces. (We could lose that much in a good sneeze!)

On the other hand, if we gain a quarter of a pound, our whole week is up in flames. Nothing but carrot sticks, forever. Bad girl.

Now, this is silly. I say, let's get happy, get healthy and get on with life!

This book is a celebration of who you are right now. If your health (and your doctor) requires you to change your eating habits and increase your exercise, by all means go for it. But . . . you still need the life-changing material in this book.

Too often, we postpone joy until we are, say, a size 10. I've *been* a size 10, and was no more joyful at that size than I am now as a size 22 Tinkerbell. "Thin" does not guarantee health, happiness or a husband. Today, and every day, you need to be assured that you are a woman of immeasurable worth and great beauty "as is," not "when."

Please understand that this business of getting on with our lives does not mean we are giving up, nor does it mean we are living in denial. It's simply an acknowledgment of the truth about dieting, exercise and good health, and an acceptance of the bodies we've been given. Really, it's more than just acceptance, it's a celebration!

The more we learn about how the human body works, the more we are discovering that "healthy" means having a healthy mind and spirit, as well as a healthy body, not to mention having a healthy sense of humor!

Throughout the pages of *"One Size Fits All" and Other Fables*, you're going to meet lots of women — more than two hundred of them — from thirty-seven states across America. They come in all sizes, from 4 to 34, all shapes, all ages, from teens to seniors, and from all walks of life. You'll laugh with them, cry with them, and applaud their insights. In fact, the dozen chapter titles are some of their favorite fables about weight, size and dieting.

Through surveys, interviews and heartfelt discussions with these wonderful, honest women, I've discovered that very few of us (even the size 4's) are happy with our bodies, particularly the amount of flesh attached thereto. Everyone expressed a desire for some encouraging words that would help them accept themselves for who and what they are, regardless of size or shape.

Each chapter is followed by interviews with experts in women's health, fitness, psychology, nutrition, fashion and publishing, who offer further insights for those of us seeking answers to questions like, "Does my size affect my health?" and "Can you be fit *and* fat?" Their responses may surprise you.

Prepare to be encouraged, my friend, because it's time to look at your beautiful body in a whole new light. It's time to embrace all of your lovable self, just as God made you.

It's time to stop crying and start rejoicing!

"There's a Thin Person Trapped Inside You"

Raise your hand if you have ever stood in front of one of those carnival mirrors that make you look thinner. I'm assuming you hustled right past the one that makes everything w-i-d-e-r, until your eyes settled on the Magic One and you took your stance.

There you were, thin. You were also eight feet tall (but a very slim eight feet). If you moved forward or back, you could create the illusion of a nice elongated neck (say, 38 inches), or the waistline of a bird. A flamingo. True, it wasn't your fantasy body, but it was a thinner one.

File that under, "Lies My Mirror Told Me."

What is it about being thin? Why have many of us longed after it with more passion than we've ever poured into our jobs, our friendships, our marriages, our lives?

My Own Journey

Growing up, I surrounded myself with words about being thin. If I close my eyes I can still see those hand-lettered signs taped all over the walls of my navy blue and yellow bedroom:

"Think Thin"
"Thin Is In, Stout Is Out"
"Loose Lips Sink Hips"

I had a little diet and exercise guide that told me I should weigh 128. At 5'9", my 145 pounds seemed obese. A more recent weight chart would have put me right at the middle of the range. I was already the perfect weight.

But that little book said I was 17 pounds overweight. I spent hours reading and re-reading it, convinced that if I thought about it long enough, a thinner body could be mine. When I blew out the candles on my birthday cake every July I had only one wish: to be thin.

You need to know that my scale hasn't registered anything close to 145 for a *long* time! In the years since then, I've traveled the yo-yo road: up, then down, then up some more, then down, then up even more. You know the routine. Maybe you've made that journey yourself.

Do you, like me, remember certain years as "thin ones" or "fat ones?" I carry around in my head an imaginary calendar, with very specific, chronological memories of my trips up and down the scale.

Take 1964. Please. Fifth grade. I was aware that I was both taller and heavier than most kids in fifth grade. I always took solace in knowing there were two other girls in my class who were bigger than I was. How ridiculous that sounds; but some of us still make such comparisons when we walk into a room full of strangers: "Oh, good! She's at least 20 pounds heavier than me!"

I'm embarrassed to admit that at my ten-year high school reunion, I scanned the room for both those classmates to see who was still the biggest. That was a "thin" year for me (remember, I had a reunion to go to), so I was the smallest of the three. For a season, anyway.

When I shot up five inches in sixth grade, my weight was suddenly distributed more evenly, and I would have qualified as "normal." Not thin, mind you, but certainly average or healthy. But that was the year I stumbled on the little book, so guess how I saw myself?

Fat.

Junior high school was where I learned how to diet, in search of that elusive "thin person trapped inside me." I had lots of company. It seems the only subjects my friends and I talked about were diets, calories, boys (which is *why* we said we wanted to be thin) and losing weight. Down two pounds — HOORAY! Up three pounds — UGH.

As recently reported in *USA Today*, child psychiatrist Ann Childress surveyed close to 1600 girls, and found that 50% of eighth grade girls had dieted. Fifty percent! Dangerous stuff, since dieting before adolescence can slow a child's growth. Childress said, "We need to educate parents on how so much of body build is genetic, so they can promote self-acceptance in kids."

If only my parents had heard that message when I was thirteen! Instead, I dieted with gusto. My friend Judy and I lived on sugarless gum, saltines and yogurt. And pizza, served with large heapings of guilt. We would "save our calories" all day, anticipating that pepperoni binge.

I remember the night we sat in front of Judy's TV, watching a beauty pageant — while eating popcorn. When the winner, Cybill Shepherd, announced that she kept herself thin by chewing gum, our faces lit up. Here was the answer!

We chewed gum constantly, certain that it kept anything evil from passing through our lips. (This did not work. We found out that gum could be parked somewhere while we were indulging in chocolate chip cookies. We also found out that chewing gum in school earned you three afternoons in the detention hall.)

Not much has changed. Women still want fashion models, movie stars and beauty queens to tell us all their diet secrets. On a recent trip to my neighborhood supermarket, I found the following two headlines on display at the check-out counter:

"Lose Weight Like a Star:
Weight Loss Secrets of Shrinking Stars."

"50 Stars' Slimming Secrets:
How They Stay So Young Looking — And YOU Can Too."

One of the many stars featured was Cher, who brought in a team of trainers at $5,000 a week, a nutritionist and a personal cook at $1,200 a week, and spent $200,000 in one year for gym equipment and related expenses.[1]

"And you can too"?

My own favorite diet advice comes from a much more authoritative source, and a very big star. Miss Piggy said, "Never eat more than you can lift."

The Truth with a capital T is this: *every woman, whatever her size or shape, is beautiful.* Fight the urge to say, "Not me!" I said that myself for years. The word "beautiful" literally means "good" or "fine," and the definition of the word includes, "a work of art."

Now, you *are* that: a unique creation, one-of-a-kind, divinely designed, a work of art. Instead of falling into the trap of defining your appearance by comparison ("I'm not as pretty as Christie Brinkley"), say, "I am the best me that I can be."

That's what being beautiful really means.

There She Is, Miss America

You are not only beautiful, you are Miss America material... and I'll prove it! *USA TODAY* published the vital statistics of the 1989 Miss America contestants, and came up with an average for each category. (I like to make things easy, so if you have even one quality that matches this list, that makes you Miss America material!).

Let's see if any of these fit you:

1. **The average Miss America is twenty-three years old.**
   (Okay, moving right along...)
2. **All the contestants are single.**
   (After all, she is MISS America. Since this is my book, I'll let you count "single again," too.)
3. **The majority of contestants have brown hair.**
   (I should raise my own hand on this one, but instead I'll confess that my blonde hair is... chemically dependent.)
4. **Most contestants also have brown eyes.**
   (With tinted contact lenses, *you* can be a brown-eyed beauty, too.)
5. **The average height for Miss America is 5'6".**
   (Surprised? I had always imagined them as very tall, like the super models, but the average height is well within the grasp of many of us. Whatever your height, it's not worth wearing tippy-toe heels to catch up!)
6. **Her average weight is 114 pounds.**
   (Uh-oh. Let's try this: I'll count it if you *ever* weighed 114, even if you shot past it in fourth grade! (Back in the good old days, Miss America 1922-23, Mary Campbell, weighed 140.[2])
7. **The average dress size is 6.**
   (Slight consolation: that's not the smallest size on the rack, there are still 2's and 4's. There are even 1's and 3's!)

8. **The average waist of a Miss America is 24 inches.**
   (I consider this unnatural. My daughter, Miss Lillian, is
   an active, adorable four-year-old. Recently, I got out a
   tape measure to see what her waist measurement might
   be. It was 18 1/2", which turned out to equal her chest
   and hip measurements too!)

You'll like the next one better:

9. **Her average shoe size is 7 1/2.**
   (Of course. She hasn't had children yet. I was ready for
   stretch marks and saggy breasts, but nobody warned me
   that my feet would swell during pregnancy and never go
   back down. I went from a dainty size 8 shoe to a defiant
   size 10 in nine months. Ah well. Small price for a baby,
   this.)

The health conscious among us will appreciate the next final
statistic:

10. **None of the contestants have ever smoked cigarettes.**
    (Gold stars and brownie points for you if you can raise
    your hand on this one.)

Here's the amazing conclusion: when these contestants were
asked to rate their physical beauty on a scale of one to ten, they gave
themselves an 8.62.

Wait a minute. A 24 inch waist, a size 6 dress, and twenty-three
years old and *still* not a "10?" When even Miss America doesn't see
herself as "perfectly" beautiful, no wonder the rest of us struggle with
our self image!

Plastic Beauty

We've all heard the tales of beauty contestants who have spent
their hard-earned money (or their parents' money) on breast
enlargement, nose reduction and other plastic surgery. "What price
beauty," we've sighed, shaking our heads.

But, models, movie stars and pageant participants aren't the *only*
women who choose such options. Many "average" women do too.
For example, in 1989, a survey among plastic surgeons found 71,000

of us wanted bigger breasts.[3] Which brings up one of many benefits of being a big woman: when I stopped dieting, I gained a bustline!

Robert Frost said, "A person will sometimes devote all his life to the development of one part of his body...the wishbone." Unfortunately, we want it both ways: tiny waist, no hips, large breasts. That's strictly glossy magazine stuff. In my whole lifetime, I have met perhaps five women who came by that combination naturally. (They, of course, hated their hair.)

That same year, 1989, another 48,000 people wanted their tummies tucked (15% were under eighteen years old – how flabby could an eighteen-year-old tummy be? – and 23% were men).

Harder to believe: 10,000 folks received fat injections,[4] a concept that escapes me completely!

Has it really come to this? Have we allowed ourselves to be turned into objects with removable, changeable parts? Are our bodies construction zones in various stages of repair, with some parts slated for demolition?

Whatever happened to the psalmist's assurance that we are "fearfully and wonderfully made?"[5]

When we look in the mirror, most of us see double chins, lines, wrinkles, blemishes, crow's feet, bags under our eyes, figure "flaws" – the list goes on and on. That's because we seldom look in a mirror unless we are looking for potential problems.

"Does my hair look okay?"

"Do I need more lipstick?"

"Is my slip showing?"

"Do I look fat in this dress?"

No wonder we find things that need fixing.

When I look in the mirror, I simply see a woman: unique, created by God, the only one quite like her. She is not "better than" or "worse than" or in need of an overhaul. She is definitely happy. (And yes, sometimes my slip is showing, too, but that's very fixable.)

When I look at you, sitting out there in the third row at one of my presentations; when I see your upturned face, full of life, ready to laugh, I do not see wrinkles, blemishes or double chins. I do not see "figure flaws." I see a beautiful woman. I see a woman who is radiant, alive, willing to learn, ready to grow, expectant, laughing and anxious to embrace all that life has to offer. You are something else!

That's not me, you may say. I'm not in your third row, I'm here at home and I'm miserable and I hate my lumpy body and radiant is not what I feel.

Understood.

But what I'm talking about transcends feelings and moves into the realm of faith in order to become fact. That radiant, alive woman is in you, even if you can't see her yet. She was in me for thirty years before I realized it, and she is in you now. And she wants out!

I don't believe for one minute that there is a THIN person trapped inside you, as our fable says, waving frantically to get out. But I do believe there is a BEAUTIFUL you trapped inside, one who was created in the image of God. He is all things beautiful, and He created and defined beauty in our world.

Surely He didn't make lovely butterflies, exquisite flowers and gorgeous sunsets, and leave out womankind, the crown of His creation?

When we stop listening to what Madison Avenue and Hollywood tell us is beautiful, and start listening to our hearts, they will not steer us wrong.

Even though we may never look like the ultra-thin models or movie stars (only 5% of us have the physiology to do so), they, poor things, will never get to look like *us*!

Look around you. Women come in all shapes and sizes, large and small, short and tall. In every home, in every workplace, in every social group, in every church, there are as many different sizes, shapes and personalities as there are women.

Thank goodness! If we all looked like Cindy Crawford, she would be out of work and the entire diet and fitness industry would collapse. (What a shame.)

Each of us is different, and those differences are good.

The Audience Speaks

When I invited audience members to be part of *"One Size Fits All" and Other Fables*, I was often surprised at who came forward to fill out my survey, because some of these women were downright thin!

My only requirement was that they be willing to share their thoughts about body confidence, especially if they were having some sort of struggle going on in their lives with weight, dieting, or body image.

I believe for every woman brave enough to step forward, ten more were thinking, "I really ought to fill out that questionnaire too!"

That means this survey can hardly be considered a scientific sampling of American women. But when it comes to speaking from the heart, these women represent us very well.

They come from all walks of life — administrators to x-ray technicians — and all stages of maturity. When they're not working or mothering, these women are busy having *fun*. Their social and leisure pursuits include everything from rollerblading to quilting to sailing to writing poetry. Once again, we are *different*; there are no stereotypes here and many surprises.

Our Above-Average Bodies

The biggest surprise was this: the average dress size turned out to be 18.35! (Does Lane Bryant carry that one?) That's much higher than the size 6 beauty contestant.

DRESS SIZES	% of those surveyed	AGE RANGES	% of those surveyed
Size 4	1%		
Size 6	4%	18–24	3%
Size 8	4%		
Size 10	5%	25–34	21%
Size 12	8%		
Size 14	6 %	35–44	43%
Size 16	11%		
Size 18	11%	45–54	23%
Size 20	14%		
Size 22	11%	55–64	8%
Size 24	10%		
Size 26	8%	65+	2%
Size 28	3%		
Size 30	1%		
Size 32	2%		
Size 34	1%		

As you can see, 72% of us wear clothing in sizes 16+, which means even the smallest town in America *should* have a decent store that features those sizes, though many don't. I was surprised to find such a large jump in percentages from size 14 to size 16 — almost double!

If you've ever felt like you were the only woman who wears a size 20, as you can see, you have lots of company. That was the most popular dress size among these many women.

200+ Women, 200+ Pages of Hope

Each woman's state of residence appears next to her name throughout the book. We have an excellent representation, with only thirteen states missing: Alaska, Delaware, Maine, Maryland, Mississippi, Montana, Nevada, New Mexico, North Dakota, Rhode Island, Vermont, West Virginia and Wyoming.

If your state is among these, why not write me and request a survey? I'll send one to you, no charge of course. When you fill it out and send it back, then I'll know what a woman from your area thinks and feels about this subject.

The most revealing question I asked women was this: "What do you hope *'One Size Fits All' and Other Fables* will include?"

Liz — you've got your job cut out for you. I've read many books about large sizes. I think yours would be a winner if it appealed more to the "normal" size audience.

Melissa from Ohio

Here's what's interesting: the "normal size" these days is actually size 12–14. And our survey respondents averaged a size 18! This book is really for every woman who has ever struggled with her body image (about 95% of us!), and should be especially encouraging for the woman who wears a size 16+.

Make me see that we're all really alike — just different sizes. Make me laugh and be more comfortable with myself. I realize size 16 isn't that large, but everyone else seems to either be a size 10 or a size 20, and I'm heading upward!

Jan from Indiana

Those of us who've either visited or resided at size 16 know just what she means. It does feel like a not-quite-big, not-quite-small size.

Since many dress stores carry only up to size 14, and shops for larger women often begin at 18W, it can be tricky. Whether you go up or down, though, you'll still be you . . . which is pretty terrific!

Give us a framework for re-thinking "same size" mentality.
                                             Carla from New Hampshire

I love the words "re-thinking" and "mentality." The mind is indeed where the changepoint occurs. I'm into "brain washing," myself: wash out the old, pour in the new!

I wish you could give a message to those who have "fatphobia."
However, my guess is that only those with some extra weight will
really read and enjoy the book.
                                             Kitty from Kentucky

Take heart! Everyone will read this book (well, at least everyone in my extended family, and forty-some people is a start!). As our surveys indicate and our own ears tell us, the majority of American women think they are overweight.

We're All In This Together

Almost a decade ago, Dr. Susan Wooley, co-director of an eating disorder clinic at the University of Cincinnati Medical College, conducted a well-known survey of 33,000 women for *GLAMOUR* magazine. She discovered that 75% of these women considered themselves overweight. Seventy-five percent! Only 25% actually were above the desired weight according to insurance charts; 25% were at just the right weight; and another 25% were underweight.[6] For all these women, and the people who love them, *"One Size Fits All" and Other Fables* will have some words of wisdom and hope.

I love to read books which are meant to make me laugh and think.
Yes, I would like to lose some weight, but I need to understand I
will never be a size 8 and I should be happy with a size 14 or 16
as long as I'm healthy. Encourage me to take care of myself—
exercise, watch fat intake, but be happy with my size.
                                             Barbara from Kentucky

Encouragement is my favorite task! Because it drains our energy and self-esteem, I'd also like to help women handle that constant nagging feeling of "I ought to be on a diet."

The process that has made sense for me is this: be happy with my size, as is. Genuinely happy. Then, exercise because I enjoy how it makes me feel, because I love doing it. Finally, moderate fats and sugars because I want to take good care of the body God has loaned me, not because I want to lose weight. That's the road to acceptance *and* health.

> *Help alleviate the focus on tiny, small, thin and help me genuinely believe, "It's what's inside that counts!"*
> Marlene from Washington

What's inside not only counts, it's the only part of us that's eternal. Most of us don't need a face-lift just a faith lift!

> *People think that only folks with lots of extra weight worry about eating issues and body image. I'm not real overweight by any means but I have a perfectionist ideal that I probably got from my mother. I would be pleased if you'd address the psychological dynamics of getting happy with your body as it is, rather than yearning for an ideal that is so hard to maintain.*
> Cindy from Illinois

I am not a psychologist, but I do know something about "getting happy," and a whole lot about dealing with perfectionism. Of this I'm sure: they are not related! A wise soul once said, "Happiness is not in things, it is in us."

> *As self-esteem boosters for more-than-perfect-size women, we need to let all people know that larger women do well at jobs, are loved, have good sex lives, dress attractively, are physically active — that we're just like everyone else, only more so!*
> Catherine from Kentucky

I love her "only more so" outlook! Here's another perspective:

> *Everyone thinks I have a great personality, but inside I am very unhappy. I wish my size didn't bother me — but it does. I hope your book will give me some answers to myself.*
> Nancy from Indiana

She is not alone. Some days I don't like my body either. But there were also days I didn't like what I saw in the mirror when I wore a size 10. (That's probably because there was a larger person trapped inside me, trying to get out!)

Time for a Change

Psychology Today conducted a survey of 30,000 men and women, asking them, "How do you feel about your appearance?"

In 1972, 25% of the women said they were dissatisfied with how they looked. In 1985, 38% of the women said they were unhappy with their appearance. At this rate, by the year 2005, each of us will be 100% miserable with our appearance!

Wouldn't it be wonderful if, after reading your book, women could look in a mirror and celebrate themselves for who they are, not for what they weigh?

Jude from South Dakota

In a word, Jude . . . yes!

My heart's desire would be for women of all shapes and sizes to live authentically, to stop making excuses or apologies, to do away with blaming others or hating ourselves because of our bodies. We can never expect others to accept who we are until *we* accept who we are.

Let me close this chapter with a true confession. I spent ten years on the radio as an on-air personality; a disc jockey, if you will. Although I couldn't see my audience, I could chat with them on the phone, meet them in person, and get some feedback along the way.

Sometimes they offered encouraging words: "I love your radio show!" And sometimes their words were hurtful: "I never dreamed you'd be overweight!" Ouch. But at least they were honest with me, and I could connect with them in some manner, face to face or by phone.

When I became a professional speaker in 1987, I found out that I loved public speaking even more than working in a radio studio. Now, with a live, in-the-flesh audience, I see their reactions immediately: laughter, surprise, nods, applause, even tears. I feel free to share very openly with them, knowing I can adapt my message to suit each situation.

But this writing thing, this nakedness on paper, without being able to watch your eyes, sense your mood, or hear your laughter — this is much scarier than standing in front of thousands of people. Writing about something as personal, and as life-changing, as the need for women to get off the diet treadmill is risky. It's not a popular view (yet), nor an easy one to live out.

My own body confidence waivers on occasion (daily!), and so it's a constant challenge to "walk my talk." Just knowing you're still with me means everything.

Begin Building Body Confidence Today

1. Do something nice for your body. Rub in a fragrant lotion from head to toe, or give yourself a facial. Take your time. You are worth it.

2. Put on your favorite outfit, head to toe. Wear make-up if you choose, and style your hair the way you like it. Now, stand in front of a full-length mirror, smile and say "Hello, Gorgeous!" Take an inventory of your favorite physical attributes. Find at least twenty.

3. Spend ten minutes reading something that feeds your soul. A book of poetry, a literary classic, whatever will inspire you. I love the book of Proverbs, which includes this verse: "Say to wisdom, 'You are my sister,'/And call understanding your nearest kin."[7]

❤ *A Women's Health Educator Speaks . . .*

Lynette Neal has been a women's health educator for more than twenty years. Her current position at Providence Milwaukie Hospital in Oregon puts her in touch with women of all shapes, sizes and levels of health.

Liz: What do you see as the most significant problem for women concerning size?

Lynette: *We have unrealistic expectations and will only be satisfied with big results. We don't seem willing to settle for a healthy middle ground. It's a perfectionist, all-or-nothing attitude that says only thin counts, and unless a diet and exercise program can guarantee us a thin body, it isn't worth it.*

Liz: What can a woman who wants to be healthier do?

Lynette: *She needs to really value herself enough to take care of herself. I don't mean lose weight. I mean get enough sleep, take time to relax, maybe get a massage, walk regularly, choose the healthiest foods she can just because they are good for her, not because she will be thinner. Our goals need to change, as well as the motivations behind them.*

Liz: What attitudes do you think need changing?

Lynette: *Women do an incredible amount of self-talking. For larger women, most of it is negative self-talk. That needs to change. And, we need to stop negating everything about our worth simply because of body size. We also need to recognize our individual strengths and build on those instead of focusing on our weaknesses.*

Liz: As a large and lovely woman, you have come to such a place of peace about this issue. What's the key?

Lynette: *Confidence. Knowing that I have value, that I make a contribution to my workplace, my family, my community.*

Liz: What other observations would you offer?

Lynette: *Large women do not allow thin women to have problems. When we see a woman with a nice figure who is complaining about her job or her marriage or whatever, we think, "Gee, you shouldn't be having any problems, look how thin you are." Body size has nothing to do with happiness, unless we erroneously choose to define it that way.*

Liz: Change is so difficult. Where do we start?

Lynette: *Ask yourself this question: "If I can't make a big change, can I make a little one? What one small step toward health could I take?"*

Liz: Why is it taking so long for women to embrace this new, healthier way of thinking?

Lynette: *Most of what we're hearing from size-acceptance advocates is fueled by anger, and is too strident, too militant to appeal to the general population of large women. Therefore, we may discount the good information they are advocating. All of us need to get to a place where big is neither better nor worse, it just is.*

"All It Takes Is a Little Willpower"

This is the fable that cuts to the quick: All it takes to lose weight, stop eating junk food, and stick to a diet is "a little willpower." The late comedienne Totie Fields said it best: "I've been on a diet for two weeks, and all I've lost is two weeks."

We repeat to ourselves over and over: "If I just had more discipline." Never mind that we went to night school while working full time, which took discipline. So what if we get our kids on the school bus every day right on time (well, almost), which takes incredible planning and execution. Forget that we saved hundreds of dollars to buy a house, said "no" to drugs, said "yes" to daily vitamins. As soon as we see that number on the scale, that flesh under our chin, we say, "I have NO willpower!" And so we begin a diet. Oh, do we feel in control of things now! Look out world; I am following this thing to the letter. Four ounces of chicken, no skin, no gravy. No flavor, either, but look at all this willpower!

Why Diets Are Disastrous

The weight loss industry smacks its corporate lips when we get a shot of willpower coursing through our veins. We're talking about those folks who give us lo-cal products, diet books and videos, fitness clubs and weight loss centers. People who benefit when our willpower weakens. It's big business in more ways than one.

In 1990, the diet industry rang up $30.2 billion in sales revenue. We bought more than $13 billion worth of diet soda alone! We spent another $3.5 billion on weight loss centers and hospital-based programs.[1] If we ever figured out how much money we've spent in our lifetime in the name of losing weight, it would probably add up to a few thousand dollars an ounce.

Today, or any day, thirty million American women are on diets of one kind or another.[2] One woman's response to just the word "diet" is telling:

> *High level of effort — low payoff. Dangerous marketing ploy — abusive to women!*
>
> Donna from Kentucky

I remember two of the early diet potions from my childhood. First there was Ayds, a chewy candy-like product that was supposed to control your appetite. It was big in the early 50's, but persisted for years. Remember the full-page ads and before and after photos? I was hypnotized by them.

Then there was Metrecal, which showed up on grocery store shelves in 1959. As is usually the case, this fad was all the rage for about two years, then faded into obscurity.[3] Even so, I can still see the television commercials featuring the Metrecal for Lunch Bunch dancing before my eyes. I was six.

"Go Where?"

Well-meaning friends and family often say, "You should go to such-and-such diet group!" There are plenty to choose from. Many of the weight-loss support groups we know today got their start around the same time. TOPS was first in 1948,[4] then Overeaters Anonymous in 1960, Weight Watchers in 1963, Diet Control Center in 1968 and so on.[5] No wonder we grew up thinking that dieting was the American way of life. According to a poll published in *USA Today*, 65% of Americans go on a diet each year. More than half of those diets only last thirty days. (Can you say "yo-yo?")

I remember my first trip to a diet organization, in 1976. (Just for the record, I weighed 150, but was still shooting for that elusive 128.)

They gave us a sheet of paper with a brick wall drawn on it. The idea was simple: for each hour that you were "legal" (don't you love that one?), you could fill in one of the bricks. Twenty-four bricks for each day, 168 bricks for each week. A brick wall between you and no willpower.

For those of us striving for perfection in our dieting, this brick wall was the ideal way to measure just how well our willpower was holding up. One tiny crumb of chocolate cake and — horrors! — an empty brick.

Even if 167 hours of my week were brimming with willpower, there was always that one empty brick staring me in the face, shouting out the terrible truth: "You just don't have enough self-control!"

No one else ever sees the brick walls we run into trying to lose weight, but it humiliates us just the same. We suffer defeat in silence, alone. We wouldn't dare tell someone else that we think this dieting thing is impossible, because we know what would be written all over their faces: "She has no willpower." So we conclude that everyone else has willpower except us.

Tuesday Night Meetings

For many of us, our mainstay was Weight Watchers. The food plans were fairly healthy, the classes upbeat, the cost was decidedly less than other options. Just one little problem . . .

> *I can learn to eat and lose weight successfully with Weight Watchers and I have lost 45–50 pounds several times. I've always gained it back, though.*
>
> Phyllis from Tennessee

Interesting how we define "losing weight successfully." Even the most "sensible" diet isn't much like our normal eating pattern. When we return to that pattern, the weight returns too. We sign up again, thinking, "this will be the time . . ."

In her book *Breaking All the Rules*, Nancy Roberts explains that the reason she kept going back to Weight Watchers again and again was because "it allows people already obsessed with food to develop, enhance and perfect that obsession." It was in fact a "winning combination of group dynamics and sanctioned obsession."[6]

How well I remember those weekly weigh-ins. Women lined up by the dozens to pay someone nine dollars for the worst news of their week. We could have found this out for free in our own bathrooms. But no, we wanted a public flogging. We wanted to be shamed into success, or have the chance to gloat if we'd had a good week.

If you've never been to such a meeting, let me give you the ground rules. At least 99% of the attendees are women. Weigh-in came right after pay-in, and was preceded by one last trip to the potty (and a "pray-in!"). Night meetings were hard for most of us because they meant an entire day of not eating. No wonder we headed for the nearest restaurant when the meeting was over!

Some people wore the same dress week after week, the flimsiest thing they owned, even in the dead of winter. Shoes always came off first — it helped to wear slip-on flats. I watched women linger at the back of the line while they unhooked belts, slipped off jackets, pulled off sweaters, the works.

One night, I stood behind a woman who had obviously had a bad week. As she got closer to the scale, sweat started popping out in little beads on her forehead. She slipped off her earrings, then her watch, then a little skinny gold necklace, two bracelets and her wedding band. (Her wedding band? How much could that weigh?) She dropped them all in her blouse pocket and got on the scale.

Poor dear. I didn't have the heart to tell her why this didn't help, especially when she gained four and a half pounds. The least I could have done was offered to hold her jewelry.

We'd Rather Die Than Diet

I asked women to tell me on the surveys "What thoughts or experiences come to mind when you think of the word 'diet'?" I was amazed to read over and over, in other women's handwriting, the exact same things I have often felt.

> *I just get a very tired feeling. A sad, frustrated, and sort of rebellious feeling. I've been on diets that took the weight off, then it came back and brought along "friends."*
>
> Pat from Wisconsin

Like the old saying goes, sometimes we get "sick and tired" of being "thick and tired." The word "frustrated" showed up on lots of surveys too.

Agony, futility, frustration, hunger, depression, loss of self-esteem.
Ada from California

Dieting also brings to mind a very specific menu. Barbara from Kentucky admits, "I hate tuna fish and I'm tired to tears of salad." Mary from Pennsylvania has an even more narrow food plan. "Dieting means you're not allowed to eat anything good."

When it comes to willpower, it seems that some people need it and others don't. Now that's not fair!

Our two sons, ages twenty-two and twenty-five, have moved back home after college graduation. They're slim and trim and can eat anything. So I catch myself thinking how fortunate they are to be able to do that.
Dorothy from Kentucky

Dorothy has hit on something there. Her sons "eat anything." In other words, they have no willpower. But it doesn't matter, because they are slim. They are the fortunate ones.

But the Dorothys of the world are expected to come up with loads of willpower simply because they are *not* "slim and trim." H-m-m.

Here's a similar story:

Dieting is a lifetime commitment I just can't handle. I wish I could control my eating like my sixteen-year-old daughter who's 5'7" and size 3.
Janet from Kentucky

Again, here's a comparison of our own bodies at age forty-plus to those of our children who have faster metabolic rates and often higher activity levels. They seldom have to worry about groceries, cooking or clean-up, and they've yet to experience the effects of aging and gravity, not to mention childbirth or decades of diet attempts.

"Won't" Power

Willpower concerning food can lead to serious problems. For many of us, exerting power over our eating habits can produce an obsessive need to control food intake which can lead to eating disorders such as anorexia nervosa and bulimia. In other words, willpower is not always a good thing.

Susan Kano, in her outstanding book, *Making Peace with Food*, lists some of the symptoms of anorexia nervosa, bulimia and chronic dieting. They include:

1. Preoccupation with dietary control; chronic attempts to eat less
2. Preoccupation with eating
3. Preoccupation with thinness/fatness and distorted body image[7]

As you can see, the common word is "preoccupation." Many women have dieted, have thought about the next meal, have wanted to lose 10 pounds. The key here is realizing how *much* those things occupy your mind, time, and activities. Willpower taken to the extreme is no power at all.

The truth is, nobody I've ever met (and liked) had endless willpower. Ugh! Who wants to hang around somebody who never bends her will to meet another's need, who never changes her mind, who never gives in to the desire of her heart? Boring!

A funny fellow named Steve Burns has the perfect solution: "Eat as much as you like — just don't swallow it." Of course, we're awfully hard on ourselves when we do swallow it.

> *I have no willpower. My "magic number" is 140, and I weigh 148. I have never been able to lose more than two pounds and it lasts a couple days!*
>
> Barbara from Ohio

Many of us identify with the "magic number" problem. We think only perfect counts, and perfect is always unattainable. Otherwise it wouldn't be perfect!

The Dreaded Treadmill

Which brings up another word that often surfaces when women talk about dieting. It's a word we repeat like a mantra, the most negative, defeating, discouraging word in American English: failure. It comes from a Latin word meaning, "to disappoint." And when we fail, the person we disappoint most is ourselves.

Pain, punishment, failure, deprived. You are on a merry-go-round of failure and you can't get off!

Martha from Ohio

There's that diet treadmill that just keeps going round and round.

Here we go again! Defeat. "Why couldn't I have kept it off?" I wonder how I could be so stupid to fall off the wagon so many times!

Peg from Kentucky

We can all identify with her frustration, even though we know "stupidity" has nothing to do with it. The problem isn't us, it's the "wagon!"

The embarrassment of gaining back lost weight cannot be understood except by someone who has been there. (I have been there!) People do a double-take when they see you and say things like, "I didn't recognize you. Have you cut your hair?" Or they just stutter, speechless. It's easy to beat yourself up when that happens.

For many of us "yo-yo's," we are aware even at the start of Diet #84 that there will be a Diet #85 someday.

Kind of like planned obsolescence — failure is programmed in at the start. When I hear about someone on or starting a diet I feel sorry for the pain and failure they are in for.

Mary Jane from Kentucky

I feel sorry for them, too, although what most just-starting dieters want us to feel is happy for them.

I've been on and off diets — hoping each one would be "IT." It is my biggest problem.

Monica from Ohio

This breaks my heart, maybe because it sounds like the old me talking. Have you ever felt like your weight was your "biggest problem?" When I think of the energy and angst we have spent on this single, narrow area of our lives it truly makes my heart ache.

Medically Supervised Failure

The diets we are willing to endure are endless in their variety, and in their ability to inflict pain.

I once was put on Dexedrine by my doctor. I went fishing with my son. He wanted to go in and get some lunch. I kept saying "just one more worm." I didn't know then that this was what we call "speed" now.

Nora from Ohio

Many of us have used pots of strong black coffee, to try and accomplish the same thing. The following story describes an experience common to many of us "diet warriors" who have tried everything.

They charged an arm and a leg for required blood work ($160), you had to pay an initial fee of $99 for registration, and after my second visit they said I needed to purchase the "maintenance package" in advance for $159. They were unprofessional, I never saw a doctor, and the nurse told me she was only part-time. They also weighed me on a different scale each of the four times I went before I became totally disgusted. I began to feel like a piece of meat being inspected and scolded or praised depending on how my week went.

Vicky Lynn from Ohio

There are plenty more tales where those came from:

I've tried Weight Watchers several times, Take Off Pounds Sensibly, Overeaters Anonymous, American Weight Loss (developed fissures), acupuncture, shots of hormone from the urine of a pregnant cow, Dr. Stillman's Diet (by the seventh day, I was ready to shoot him too!). In recent years, I have learned to be comfortable with myself—no more diets.

Joyce from Virginia

Facing the Bathroom Scale

Those of us who diet at home can be just as ritualistic as "professional dieters." Some women weigh themselves three, four, five times a day. Only one time counts, though, and that's the weigh-in that takes place first thing in the morning.

And, I mean *first* thing: right after a trip to the bathroom, and right before coffee. It's that little "window of opportunity," the thinnest moment in a woman's day.

Fanatics take a shower first to wash off all that heavy dirt. The next step, by necessity, is blow-drying your hair to get out all those pounds of water. Now you approach the scale, totally nude, completely empty, your most svelte self. You check the "0" setting. If the needle is directly over the "0," that's good. If it's ever so slightly to the left, that's even better. Next, you step on the scale, and start moving around. Where is that light spot? Ah. Finally, the last two steps that women of all sizes take: we exhale (air must weigh something), and then we pull in our tummies, the theory being that if you can't see it, it won't weigh anything. (Or, for some of us, so we can see the numbers!)

If we've lost a pound, we celebrate and eat something. If we've had a gain, we console ourselves and eat something. That's dieting the American weigh.

Some of My Best Friends Are Yo-Yo's

When someone tells me they've lost such-and-such pounds on a diet, my next question is always, "How long have you kept it off?" The effectiveness of any weight loss program should be determined by longevity, not how much we can lose or how fast we can lose it. By that measure, the liquid diets would fare pretty well.

Oprah Winfrey showed us on national television how easy it is to lose 67 pounds, and how even easier it is to gain it back.

Read my lips: *She* did not fail! The *diet* failed her!

Oprah has been, and continues to be, a wonderful role model for all women, but especially for the plus-size woman. She dealt a crushing blow to the liquid diet craze, not just for OptiFast, but for all the hospital and physician-based programs, as well as the across-the-counter versions. According to the *Wall Street Journal*, by September 1992, Ultra Slim-Fast sales were down 45% from the year earlier. DynaTrim sales were down 65%. People were discovering what Oprah already knew: Very low calorie diets don't work.

Naturally, any weight loss organization will tell you about their success stories. There are always a few people willing to forgo health and self-acceptance in the name of thinness. But the research statistics released in April 1992 by the National Institute of Health are not pretty: 90–95% of those who lose weight through a low calorie diet *will* gain back most of their weight within two years, and *all* of it within five years.[8] That puts the success rate at about 7%. One five-year study in Denmark logged only a 3% success rate.[9]

The insurance world would call that a poor risk. At the track, it would be a long shot. In medicine, it might be called malpractice.

When I dropped three dress sizes through strict dieting in 1982, I landed at a nice size 10-12, 160 pounds. Was I happy with that? Naturally not, it still sounded fat. It looked mighty slim, but it sounded fat. By then, I had raised my goal weight to a more "reasonable" 135. Forget the elusive 128; now, I was shooting for 135. At 5'9". Sure.

The scale never budged. A pound or two, but mostly 160, 161, 159, 162, 160, for two full years of dieting. I still have the weigh-in cards to prove it. If I was down a half-pound, I drew a smiley face. Good girl. When the scale crept up 3/4 of a pound, I made a firm red line, like I used to make in league bowling when I wasn't doing well and wanted to tell myself, "I'm starting over as of right here."

I kept that weight off very simply: I ate almost nothing. One meal a day, maybe two. Constant weigh-ins. I had a red patent leather belt from my "fat" days that I would try on as a reminder of where my waist would return to if I wasn't careful.

Two solid years of being legal, good, and righteous. Make that self-righteous. I was convinced if I could do this, anyone could. Weight was all a matter of willpower, I thought, and women who were fat ate too much. Period.

Oh, Lizzie. I was only delaying the inevitable. In the spring of 1984 I finally wearied of toting my plastic scale with me everywhere, of visualizing a pack of playing cards to measure a chicken breast, of eating everything with artificial sweetener and imitation butter. I tired of trying to get to 135. Heck, I'd even raised my goal to 145 by then, the weight I'd weighed all through high school, when 145 seemed fat to me.

Dr. Kathy Johnson, a New York psychiatrist, believes that some women "need a number, an outside source, to validate that they're doing okay."[10] I was not doing okay, because my scale was not telling me what I wanted to hear.

When I went back to normal eating — and I do mean normal, not pigging out, not stuffing my face, not three junk food meals a day — I gained back my weight at a steady one pound per week. That train chugged down the track way past the point where I had started my diet two years earlier.

Was my diet a success? I think not. Most research on yo-yo dieting now concludes that I would have been better off if I had never dieted at all. As Dr. Adriane Fugh-Berman of the National Women's Health Network says, "Yo-yo dieting is for yo-yos."[11]

Diet Defined

To be truly successful, a diet would:

1. Contain easily available, naturally healthy foods
2. Be served in quantities sufficient for your body's needs and your appetite's satisfaction
3. Produce a high level of pleasure, good for a lifetime of eating

If you have shared anything remotely like my own experiences, chances are good that you did not fail your diet, your diet failed you. Especially if it:

1. Consisted of expensive, chemical-laden substitute foods
2. Was served in tiny quantities sufficient for the body and appetite of a field mouse
3. Produced no level of pleasure whatsoever (Art Buchwald said of liquid diets, "The powder is mixed with water and tastes exactly like powder mixed with water.")

That's not a diet, that's purgatory. Or worse. Dolores hit the nail on the head when she defined the word "diet":

Deprivation, denial, punishment, sentencing, lack of trust, lack of freedom, lack of choice, embarrassment, explaining why I'm not eating, people saying "Oh, good . . ."
                                                        Dolores from New York

My hat is off to women who have successfully removed the word D-I-E-T from their vocabularies:

That is a four-letter word and we don't talk like that in our house.
                                                        Gwyn from Ohio

How exciting that she may also have a family who is learning about the ill effects of dieting. Many young girls are getting interested in dieting as early as age eight. They need a mom with compassionate concern to teach them that young girls should never diet.

> *[Dieting] doesn't work and it is not a major religion! Nor does it make you superior if you succeed.*
>
> Diana from Kentucky

I was the queen of self-righteousness when I lost weight. It was disgusting really, very us versus them in nature. I honestly thought that anyone who put their mind to it could do it. It was so simple, I reasoned. Just eat less and exercise more. Anybody who wasn't successful with this easy plan was . . . was . . . was . . . uh . . . normal. (Finally, I figured that out!)

> *A diet is something you do to war criminals while you keep them in bamboo cells.*
>
> Janet from Virginia

Sounds like the bread-and-water diet, one of civilization's oldest. We all know the word "diet" just means the food you eat, but in the last century it has come to carry a much more definitive, and more negative, connotation.

> *The word "diet" is like the word "problem." It doesn't belong in the English language. I consider myself to have "challenges and opportunities" only!*
>
> Vicki from Wisconsin

Getting Off the Diet Treadmill

When I talk about doing away with dieting, some women get almost fearful looks on their faces. If you've dieted off and on much of your life, the thought of never doing it again *is* scary.

> *I have retrained myself not to diet, but to make conscious decisions about what I put in my mouth. Diets don't work!*
>
> Lisa from Illinois

Note that this was a deliberate move away from the dreaded "D" word. Decisions, yes; dieting, no.

I have finally reached a point of being good to my body, nutritionally, emotionally and physically.

LaDonna from Oregon

This is a woman who has learned to properly care about and for herself. Here are some specific suggestions for doing that:

Eat nutritionally and keep fats to a minimum. Balance proteins and carbohydrates and give your body enough water to allow natural body function.

Lauren from Pennsylvania

Then, there's my favorite way to reduce:

Just "diet" from negative people, and you'll be happy!

Maria from Arizona

I heard from an eighteen-year-old reader of *Big Beautiful Woman* magazine who shared her journey to self-acceptance:

To me, size isn't everything. Three years ago I wouldn't say that. Now some of my friends tell me that they wish they were as comfortable with their bodies as I am with mine.

Carly from Missouri

How wonderful that she learned that lesson at such a young age. Some of us take a little longer, but we can get there. Elaine was released out of diet purgatory by (surprise! surprise!) her doctor:

One day he said to me, "When are you going to realize you're always going to be like this and quit worrying about it. You're healthy and your husband loves you—so quit worrying!" That freed me, and I don't diet and I'm still healthy!

Elaine from Ohio

The key words are: "happy" and "healthy." We must focus the power of our will toward achieving those two important goals —

genuine health, genuine happiness — and sell those food scales and bathroom scales at our next yard sale.

Many women are not willing to take such steps because they see it as "giving up." This is not giving up! It is getting off the diet treadmill and "getting on" with a healthier approach to eating, to movement, to life. It is also doing away with denial, and embracing reality with a grateful heart.

Just think: we might find out what it's like to live that "normal" life we've often longed for, without worrying about what we'll be having (or *not* having) for lunch!

Begin Building Body Confidence Today

1. Banish the word "diet" from your vocabulary. Get rid of "reducing," "weight loss" and "willpower" while you're at it. (If it's any consolation, these terms are *not* in the Bible!)

2. Throw out your bathroom scale, calorie counting guides, and fad diet books. Instead buy one good "healthy eating" cookbook. No food plans allowed!

3. If your friends start talking about diets, change the subject. If they start criticizing you or anyone else for gaining weight, change friends!

❤ A Nurse Speaks . . .

Anne Khol, N.D., R.N., has a bachelor's degree in psychology from Michigan State University and a doctorate of nursing from Case Western Reserve University in Cleveland. She is currently director of community health education for Sparrow Hospital in Lansing, Michigan.

Liz: Weight gain among women is on the way up. Why?

Anne: *Two reasons: Women are less active. The day-to-day work that we do requires much less physical activity than, say, a hundred years ago. We used to beat our rugs; now we have a high-powered vacuum. We used to knead bread; now we use bread machines (or we buy it at the store). We are not working our large muscle groups all day long, and we lead far more sedentary lives.*

The second reason is: The fashion industry has chosen to use very tall, thin models. This keeps American women constantly dieting to try and fit those clothes. We lose weight, we buy new clothes. We gain the weight back, we buy new clothes. By the time we lose again, the old clothes are out of style, so we buy new clothes. Madison Avenue loves yo-yos!

Liz: What's the problem with dieting?

Anne: *Research keeps telling us that dieting makes you fatter. Dieting itself is the problem. When you think diet, you think about calorie restriction, unfortunately. Not healthy eating, just less eating. Such dieting means you lose lean body weight, you lose muscle, and so your metabolic rate slows down. If you are an educated person in this regard, you will never "diet."*

Liz: You mean it takes more than "willpower?"

Anne: *[Laughs] All the "will" in the world can't fight your body's natural tendencies! Our bodies are designed to protect us from starvation, so calorie reduction will make the body store fat, not burn it. Eating less food tampers with the body's natural regulator, and we are depriving ourselves of what we really want and need to eat.*

Liz: How can we attune ourselves to our bodies' needs?

Anne: *We have to make a conscious effort to re-educate ourselves. The truth is, when we crave chocolates or sweets, our body is asking for more complex carbohydrates —bread, pasta, potatoes. By paying attention to hunger cravings, giving your body real food packed with vitamins, minerals and complex carbohydrates, over time you can become more discerning, as well as genuinely satisfied. It's also important to drink enough fluids. Your body needs at least 64 ounces (8 glasses) of liquids a day to replenish what your body uses — more if you exercise. If we don't provide liquid nourishment, our bodies will signal for more food to meet that need. We are reaching for food when what our body wants is water!*

Liz: Is food the real issue?

Anne: *No. Exercise is the real issue. Not only does it raise the metabolic rate, it improves your mood and cognitive processes, helps you handle stress and enhances how you feel about yourself. It improves muscle tone and skin tone too! Understand that basic changes in metabolic rate through exercise take more than a year. But the benefits begin immediately.*

Liz: You are certainly a well-educated, successful woman who also happens to be big and beautiful. What are your tips for success?

Anne: *Recognize your unique skills and abilities, and make them known. Don't settle for less. And, dress the part! Put on makeup, spend some time on your appearance. Thin women have to do this, too, so good grooming isn't limited to large women.*

Liz: As a Christian, do you think size is a spiritual issue?

Anne: *To me, it's a question of stewardship. I think it is wrong to diet, and to do so harms our bodies. When the Bible talks about the body being God's temple, I don't think it means,*

"Watch your weight!" I believe it means watch what you are putting into your body—is it healthy or not? And, do you exercise it? God commanded Adam to work by the sweat of his brow. [Laughing] Maybe we need to sweat more!

"You're Just Big Boned"

Dem bones, dem bones, dem BIG bones. . . that's what the problem must be! I even had a doctor tell me that once: "Liz, you're not really fat, you're just big boned." Then, when he had to do a chest x-ray, he came out from behind the screen and said with a look of surprise, "You have small bones, Liz!"

I've known my bone size for years, because I can circle my wrist with my thumb and middle finger, one of the ways you measure how big your bones really are (or aren't!).

Of course, when I was growing up and looking at those insurance charts, I liked the ranges for "large-boned" people better! But the truth is, I inherited long, thin bones with plenty of cushion. That's how my family is built.

One Big Happy Family

I grew up in a large family, or as an only child, depending on how you view things. Most of my brothers and sisters had graduated and gone on to college by the time I was a preschooler. My five siblings are all between nine and nineteen years older than me. Imagine my parents' surprise when, three months before they both turned forty-three, along came this third little girl, a sixth child! Just for the record, I tipped the hospital scales at a nice, normal seven pounds, eight ounces.

The Amidons are, in the truest sense of the word, one big happy family. We're all tall, for starters. And, I don't think I'll be doing my dear brothers and sisters any disservice to say that we've all struggled with weighty issues over the years. I've probably done the yo-yo routine with more gusto, but we've all taken turns going up and down.

Here's the logical question: Am I large because I come from a family of larger people? If so, is it genetics? Lifestyle? Psychological makeup? Learned behavior? Something in the tap water?

In our surveys, 57% of us indicated we have at least one large parent, and 47% have a sibling that's our size (and remember, we received surveys from many smaller women too). If "big bones" run in your family, here are four possible explanations we hear from others (or say to ourselves). All four are grounded in fact, though all four may not fit your situation (or mine).

1. Your family's eating and exercise habits were poor.

Children do model their parents' behavior, as well as that of their older sisters and brothers. If indeed our food choices were unhealthy (and this is a big "if," but it's possible) and if exercise was not encouraged in the family, then this might be a legitimate contributing factor to our size.

Can we unlearn such things? It would be challenging, but yes, it could certainly be done.

2. You've dieted so much over the years that now your metabolic rate has been lowered.

Dieting patterns can be modeled too. My sisters and I were always going on one diet or another. Starvation seemed to work best. We each found our own favorite groups: Weight Watchers, Overeaters Anonymous, and Lean Line. For my sisters in the 50's and for me in the 60's, dieting was a way of life.

My yo-yo experiences have taken me farther both ways than either of my sisters, and although I'm the youngest, I'm also the largest. Have I just incurred more metabolic changes through severe dieting? Maybe.

Dr. Kelly Brownell from the University of Pennsylvania describes dieting-induced obesity:

> During each diet, lean body mass is lost, but is replaced with fat, as weight is regained. Fat tissue is metabolically less active, therefore the metabolic rate slows further. It takes longer to lose weight each time, and the weight is regained much faster.[1]

Sound familiar? I have often wondered what might have happened if I had quit dieting and focused on healthy, normal eating and exercise when I was back at 160 pounds.

It doesn't take a medical genius to see what happens around us every day: friends or family members go on diets, lose weight, gain it back, and are now ten pounds heavier than when they started. That is the precise path to "dieting-induced obesity."

   3. *Family members share the same psychological weaknesses that lead to addictions, with food being the family "drug of choice."*

No doubt about it, we all like to eat. But, eating compulsively is something else again. Compulsive overeating means to eat without thinking about what we are consuming. We stuff food in quickly without really tasting it or even caring how much or even what it is we're eating. We are responding to *mouth* hunger instead of *stomach* hunger.

The feeling is loss of control. Not the rational kind, like when you're eating a brownie and telling yourself, "I really don't need this!" Compulsive eating happens outside of rational thought. You literally cannot stop yourself.

Listen carefully now: It's possible to be fat and not be a compulsive overeater. It's also possible to be of average weight and eat very compulsively. Many of us are made to feel that, if we are big, we must be compulsive overeaters. This is simply not always the case.

The common assumption is that all large people overeat from the time they get up until the time they go to bed. Not so! In study after study, research has shown that large people eat less food or equal amounts of food than thin people.

Nobody believes this, so I'll say it again: Ten out of eleven recently conducted research studies indicate that large people eat *smaller* portions and often *fewer* meals than thin people do. Yet when a large person sits in a restaurant eating a normal meal, people may stare, shake their heads and look disgusted. (This is not my imagination — ask any large person if they've had this experience.) A thin woman will seldom solicit a second glance from anyone, even if she's tearing into a gigantic banana split topped with six dips of ice cream!

I've often said to people, "Please spend a day with me and watch what I eat: three meals, few snacks, lots of fruit and other healthy choices." Their lips will say, "Really?" but their eyes say, "No way, Liz. You must eat a dozen doughnuts for breakfast!" Sorry, but not so.

The truth is I have inherited genes that control how my body processes food. Through regular exercise and normal, healthy eating, I may be able to improve that metabolic rate somewhat. But I was created to be a tall, full-bodied, light brown-haired, blue-eyed, long-legged, short-waisted woman.

Which brings us to the fourth possible reason why I come from a big happy family:

4. *We are physiologically and genetically disposed to be bigger.*

Statistics speak clearly to this. Children with one large parent have a 40% chance of being large. Having two large parents doubles that to an 80% chance of being large. A child with thin parents has only a 7% chance of being fat. Environment? Nope. A study of 540 adopted men and women found their weights most closely matched their biological, not their adoptive, parents.

Big Beautiful Woman magazine's recent health survey of hundreds of readers weighing 40 pounds or more over their range on the weight charts revealed this amazing statistic: 99% of them had one or two large-size parents! And 98% of them had one or two large-size grandparents![2] Those of us who've been saying, "It's all in the genes" now have further proof that it's not in our collective imagination. It's also worth noting that of those large parents, only 10% had high blood pressure, only 5% suffered from diabetes and a mere 3% suffered from heart disease.[3]

Let me demonstrate how much being "genetically disposed to be bigger" scares some people. In 1990, *NEWSWEEK* magazine reported that of two hundred New England couples who were surveyed concerning genetic tests during pregnancy, 11% of them said they would abort an unborn baby simply for being predisposed to obesity.[4]

When I share that statement with my audiences, they always gasp. Well they should.

I love my big, beautiful family and every gene they gave me. I'm so thankful my mother, at forty-three, took a chance for both of us and brought me into this world!

Like Mother, Like Daughter

One of the women who completed our survey told us she often heard this from her mother: "You have your great-grandmother's shape." Mom may be right! Look at your own family tree, then look in the mirror. When I stand nude in front of a full-length mirror (and I'll be honest, I don't ever do this for hours at a time), I see my mother's round tummy. I only had two children, and she had six, but that shape is very familiar. As we've heard and said many times, "A girl will look like her mother in twenty years."

In my case, since I favor my father physically, I also see him when I look in the mirror. Often, we're pleased with our heritage and with the family genes that go along with it:

I'm a big-boned German descendant. My lab values are normal, I walk when the weather is nice, I enjoy people and recognize that I'm a great wife, mother, and friend. I like living.

Marilyn from Missouri

What a sense of peace and balance she's come to! Some of us get mixed feelings when we see our family staring back at us in the mirror:

When my mom lost a lot of weight for health reasons, she gave me a lot of her clothes. When I put one dress on and looked in the mirror, I had turned into my mother! She is lovely, but I'm not ready to be her.

Sandy from Michigan

In her book *The Hungry Self*, Kim Chernin talks about daughters for whom "the act of eating will be fraught with peril. With every bite she has to fear that she may become what her mother has been."[5]

This issue of weight and family is a very sensitive one, especially between mothers and daughters. Sometimes the daughter wants her mom to feel better about herself:

> *I hope [you can] inspire my mother to accept herself for what she is and see that she is just great no matter what size she is (she is only a size 14–16 — not bad for a fifty-five-year-old grandmother!).*
>
> Robin from Ohio

Not bad for anybody, I'd say! More often, it's a thin mother agonizing over a larger daughter:

> *My daughter has more of a significant weight problem [than I do] and I hope to share this [book] with her.*
>
> Pat from New Jersey

Following my presentations, I'm often approached by tearful mothers who have large, lovely daughters at home. "I wish she could meet you!" they say. "My daughter just hides at home, and I want her to see she can enjoy life and be successful even though she is big like you are."

Time for a true confession. When I call myself "big" or "bountiful" or "large," it feels good, it feels positive. When a thin woman says "big like you are," I must fight the urge to feel offended. I know that's silly, but it's also the truth. Self-acceptance is a process, an ongoing challenge, day in and day out. I now feel much less "inner bristling" when someone else acknowledges my size. After all, there it is. It's merely a fact, not an accusation, and I've already brought up the subject myself.

Voices from the Past

Perhaps one of the reasons we bristle when someone mentions our size is that we've heard it all before, many years ago. Child psychologists agree that our self-image is formed in the first five years of life. In the years that follow, we continue to hear, again and again, the messages we received at a very young age.

If you were to play back those tapes in your head, those self-talk conversations that shape how you feel about yourself, whose voices would be on those tapes? And what would they be saying? I asked women to tell me, "What comments do you receive about your size, and who says them?" Everyone from family members to strangers has made comments about our bodies. Which of these groups makes the most remarks, the majority of them negative? Sorry, Mom. You win.

We mothers are blamed for everything under the sun these days, from our children's low self-esteem to their poor marks in school. I'm not here to provide fuel for the guilt trip every mother embarks on when she checks out of the delivery room. (Remember, I'm a mother too!) Nor am I anxious to blame your own mother for the way you feel about yourself. Such finger-pointing is non-productive, even dangerous.

You're an adult now. The finger of responsibility points in your direction. You can choose to keep repeating those old negative messages, or you can choose how you feel about your body and yourself.

But let's be realistic. You can't erase a tape you can't locate. A therapist or counselor might help some of us find the source of those "old tapes." Meanwhile, by listening to others who struggle as we do, we may hear negative recordings similar to ours and begin to push our own "erase" button.

Pushing the Playback Button

I want to share with you the various messages, the scripts that women are still able to recite for us. Some are old scripts, things we've heard since childhood. Many contain new phrases, feedback that wasn't sought but was offered nonetheless as people around us reacted to our size, weight or body shape.

We'll let Mother get it out of her system first:

When I wear pants, my mother calls me "Thunder Thighs," or calls the pants, "sausage casings."

Jane from Wisconsin

Many mothers would never dream of being so direct. They make their point in more subtle ways:

My mom said, "You should lose weight — you'd feel better — it's for your own good!"

Linda from Ohio

Now, does that sound like a mother, or what? That "for your own good" stuff was practically a maternal litany that followed everything she ever told us. If her plea to "do it for your own good" doesn't work, Mother can always move to the "do it for your kids" approach, combining shame *and* guilt:

> *My mom said: "You should lose weight for your health and think of your kids. What will happen to them if you are sick or dead?"*
> Connie from Wisconsin

If you don't have children, another angle might be, "Watch it, or you'll lose your husband's interest."

Or, maybe this will sound familiar:

> *Mom has always told me I am heavy. I've always been compared to my smaller sister.*
> Heidi from Michigan

Some mothers send mixed messages:

> *There was a constant battle with her over my weight. On the one hand, I was always too fat. On the other hand, every time I did something she liked (making the cheerleading squad in junior high), I got special dinners and pies and cakes as rewards. I was terribly confused.*
> Diane from Tennessee

Let's face it, mothers are sometimes hard to please. They know us so well, watched us grow up, genuinely love us and want only the best for us.

> *I am staring at yet another size 6 petite knit (of all things) suit that my size 4 petite mother has bought for me and said, "With a little effort you could fit into this!"*
> Debra from Kentucky

Forgiveness is your best response, because in almost every case, our mothers really did mean well. The truth is, their own struggles with body image colored everything they ever said to us about our bodies.

I was fortunate to have a father who always found some kind words to say to me about my appearance. That's why I found these comments about fathers discouraging:

Having been "big" for about twenty years, my dad has called me "Lard."

Marcia from South Dakota

I've been fat since age thirteen. Father always looked at me as though he was disgusted.

Monica from Ohio

My dad called me "Bertha Butt."

Sonya from Kentucky

Our siblings like to be helpful, too, like Marcia's brother who asked: "What tent and awning store did you buy that dress from?"

It Rhymes with Cat, Sat, and Pat

Those of us with children often receive some weighty comments, too, though our children's innocence makes such observations less threatening, even laughable.

My children say, "Look Mommy, she's bigger than you!"

Gail from Texas

When my three-year-old son saw an ad on TV for an exercise video that supposedly produces "buns of steel," he said, "Mom, you need that!"

Pamela from Kentucky

One mother shared this common experience:

One of my son's friends made a derogatory comment about my weight. The painful thing about the incident was that I hurt for my son — the realization that his friends laughed at his mother — the embarrassment he might feel because his mom was fat.

Rosanne from Kentucky

I had something similar happen at church when I had nursery duty. A sweet little three-year-old boy said, "You're fat!" And I said,

"You're right!" Then I laughed and he laughed and we went right on tossing a ball back and forth. In that very brief exchange, he learned that fat is not a bad word, any more than "tall" or "short" or "thin" are bad words. They are descriptive words, perfectly appropriate. He also learned that I am already aware of my size and feel okay about it.

Fat becomes a "loaded" word when it's said in a derogatory way, or if it's said in combination with other words that do have a negative connotation. You know them all: "Fat and lazy!" "Fat and stupid!" "Fat and ugly!" "Fat slob!" You can even have a "fat chance" of doing something (which means the same thing as having a "slim chance!?").

We've chosen many words to describe our own bodies. Some of them are affectionate, even funny. Some are a thin veneer for a lot of heartache. When I asked women to tell me, "What words come to mind when you think of your body?" here were some of their responses. First, the funny ones: Heavy duty cutie. Wide load. Hidden valleys. Gravity-bitten.

The painfully honest ones: *Disgust. Disappointment. Embarrassment. Frumpy. Old, fat and gray!*

The practical ones: *Shade in the summer. Warmth in the winter. A wonderful piece of machinery. It washes up nicely and never shrinks.*

The descriptive ones: *An apple on a stick. Shaped like Mr. Peanut. Vertically Impaired — (I'm short). The Goodyear Blimp.*

The positive ones: *Soft, sensual, warm, comforting, sexy. Big and powerful. Strong, big, beautiful, voluptuous. Renoiresque, luscious.*

Our response to our bodies is, as you can see, all over the map. Those of us who love to display our wit will usually look for a funny way to describe ourselves.

I especially love the word, "luscious." A wonderful therapist in Wisconsin organized a workshop she called "Lifestyles of the Large and Luscious." Sadly, only one woman was willing to sign up. Why? Probably because so few of us see ourselves as "luscious."

Size Is Not the Issue

The amazing thing to me was this: if you covered up the dress sizes listed at the top of the surveys and just looked at the answers, they were almost identical *no matter what the woman's dress size*!

The 4's, the 14's and the 24's all said pretty much the same things: "Flabby thighs, big hips, too much tummy."

One woman wrote that her body is "still a little too plump." She wears a size 6. I'd always mistakenly assumed it was just us big girls who struggled; was I surprised to find that the problem is systemic!

When *USA TODAY* asked 8,000 readers to "grade" their bodies, 40% of both men and women gave themselves a C. That's a passing grade, but it's not honor roll material.

The newspaper survey also asked them to list what they liked about their bodies specifically, and what they didn't like. Here's how the women responded:

Women Liked MOST:	Women Liked LEAST:
1. Eyes	1. Stomach
2. Face	2. Buttocks
3. Hair	3. Legs

Above the neck, we're happy. From the waist down, we're miserable. That may be in part because we spend thirty minutes or more every day on the features we like.

Our hair is cut, styled, colored, permed, washed, set, curled, straightened, as well as combed several times a day. Our faces are scrubbed, creamed, massaged, waxed, masked, and covered with makeup almost daily. Our eyes are tweezed, lined, shadowed, and for many of us, aided by glasses or contact lenses. For the most part, we're happy with our face and hair (as well we should be, considering what we invest in them!).

The stomach, buttocks and legs are a problem for one simple reason: that's where fat deposits land first. How does that favorite saying go? We're "built for comfort, not for speed?" Women are indeed built with childbearing capabilities, and the area of our bodies where we carry that precious cargo is the stomach, buttocks and legs.

I'm Not Fat, I'm Expecting

This is the truth: I loved being pregnant! For the first time in my life, I didn't go around trying to hold in my stomach. For a season I had a bustline that actually matched my hips. . . such balance! I felt good from head to toe and only craved healthy foods (fresh pineapple and whole wheat crackers). People told me how radiant and beautiful

I was, patted my tummy, told me my ankles looked great (until the 9th month) and in general made me feel terrific about my body.

Of course, after the delivery all that ground to a halt. Six weeks later people were still asking me, "When are you due?" The "going home from the hospital" outfit I bought continued to hang in the closet with the tags still dangling from the sleeves. Suddenly my large, lovely body was supposed to be slimmer and trimmer again, as if nothing ever happened. Ha.

If you've given birth, you know what takes place. Things expand. Not just your abdomen, either. My hands and feet were permanently changed after two pregnancies only twenty months apart. Let me tell you, for the joy of having Matthew and Lillian in my life, I'm happy to buy bigger shoes and have my rings re-sized!

My friends all said, "Think of the weight you'll lose after you deliver! All that water, all that baby, it'll be twenty-five or thirty pounds, easy!" As soon as I could walk to the nurse's station I climbed on that big white scale to find out how I'd done on the have-a-baby diet.

It couldn't be right. I'd only lost five pounds! How can you have an eleven pound twelve and a half ounce baby and only lose five pounds? (Did they put some back?)

Needless to say, I was full of water. Soon it started flowing and I quickly lost about thirty pounds. My total gain was thirty-five — not bad for a baby that size. But I still came out of the whole thing with fuller, droopier breasts, a rounder tummy, bigger hips and thicker thighs. Those extra five pounds all went to the places we women supposedly hate: stomach, buttocks and thighs. And since I was big before I got pregnant, there was already lots of cushion in those three places. By saying we don't like these parts of our bodies, we're really saying, "I don't like being shaped like a woman!" Today's fashion models are usually young women — still girls really, at twelve and thirteen — with flat chests, flat tummies, no hips, no buttocks. They are, in fact, shaped pretty much like young boys. Older models, who fight like mad to compete with these young girls, must diet and exercise vigorously to keep themselves flat, sleek and bulge-free. It's not surprising that the female fashion world introduces men's suits, ties and shirts about every five years (I never see ordinary women wear those outfits, just models and actresses on TV). Those women look great in male clothing because that's the body they have to work with.

In my family, we're curvy. My mother's yearbook called her "buxom." Great word. It means, "full-bosomed, healthy, plump, cheerful and lively." In 1929, the year my mother graduated, that was a *compliment!*

Now, I'm watching to see how the family genes hold up. Just twenty months after giving birth to Matthew, I welcomed Miss Lillian Margaret Higgs into my life. Compared to her brother she was a little petite thing, just ten pounds, three and three quarter ounces.

Will Lillian also be a big, beautiful woman in a narrow, nervous world? Hard to say. Although doctors say that babies triple their birth weight in the first year, both of mine held steady for a long time. They grew at a nice, slow, steady pace, and soon were right in the normal range. Only time will tell whether they will be "big boned" too.

The Gift of Life

From my own observations, I've concluded most young girls don't feel good about their bodies because they have mothers who don't feel good about their own bodies. Many times, unhappy mothers project their own body dissatisfaction onto their daughters, saying, "Don't get fat (like me)! I don't want you to suffer (like I did)!" And so a new diet treadmill is set up for the next generation.

Whether she turns out to be model-thin or mama-size, I can guarantee you Lillian will be loved, hugged, encouraged, praised and made to feel as absolutely beautiful as possible in this house. I know the world will give her a different message, the media will berate her at any size, her friends will be talking diets by her eighth birthday, and someday some jerk might tell her he could really love her if she'd "just lose a little weight." I know all that may be in her future.

But here at home she will find a haven, a resting place. Within these walls, her mother, her first role model, is busy living and loving her own full life. A life without apology for my genes, my choices or my body. This is the Liz-that-is. Whatever size or shape Lillian turns out to have, it's my fervent prayer that she will accept it, even embrace it as God's gift to her.

In a year or two, she will be old enough to read this book. In ten years, she'll be embarrassed to tears that she's in it! I can hear her now: "Aw, Mom!" Between those two stages, I'd like to put this in writing for her, and for all our daughters:

Miss Lillian:

Daddy and I love you. God loves you. And people will love you — the moment you begin to love yourself.

With all my heart,

Mama

Begin Building Body Confidence Today

1. Forgive your family. Any negative messages they may have given you about your body cannot easily be forgotten, but they can be forgiven. In the process, their power to hurt you will diminish. When those memories come to mind, immediately respond, "I forgive you."

2. Forgive yourself. Each of us is doing the best we can with what we've been given every day of our lives. Relax and extend grace to yourself, as you do to others.

3. Embrace your genetic heritage. Concentrate on the things you really *do* like that have been passed down to you. If you see your own physical traits in your children, fight the urge to say, "You look like me, poor thing!" Instead, say "I'm so glad you got my _____!"

❤ An OB/GYN Speaks . . .

Dr. Harriette "Robin" Smith graduated from the University of Louisville School of Medicine and is board certified by the American College of Obstetrics and Gynecology. She has practiced medicine since 1982, most currently at the Louisville Women's Centers.

Liz: What are some special health concerns of larger women?

Robin: *As a rule, their cardiovascular status is not as good because they are not as active. Often their muscle tone isn't great, either, for the same reason. Large patients are more inclined to be diabetic, and have more of a tendency toward high blood pressure.*

Liz: How do those things affect pregnancy?

Robin: *The placenta is a vascular organ, where the exchange of maternal and fetal blood occurs — it's where you put in the good stuff and take out the bad. If the patient has elevated blood sugar, the babies tend to be large. Large infants can be trickier to deliver, and you'll find an increase in the number of cesarean-sections and birth trauma. If the placenta gets prematurely old or stressed because of diabetes or high blood pressure, then there's a risk for stillbirths and for growth retardation. Also, oxygen transfer is not as good.*

Liz: Good grief! Do you have any good news for the large woman who wants to give birth?

Robin: *Absolutely. If you're healthy, you're going to do fine in your pregnancy. I have just as many gorgeous babies from big people as I do from skinny ones. Thin people sometimes smoke or have poor eating habits, so thinness is no guarantee of an easy delivery or a healthy baby.*

Liz: What about women who gain weight during pregnancy and then can't lose it?

Robin: *I see a lot of that! Once you've stretched the abdominal muscles to term size, it's pretty hard to get that muscle tone back. You really have to work at it, and you are usually busy tending that baby. Everything changes: your life style, your eating and sleeping habits, everything. You have to face the fact that you will never have your high school waist again. In pregnancy your ribs expand, your feet expand, all your weight-bearing structures change. And they should! You can't fight Mother Nature. Look what we get out of the process: a wonderful new person! Those body changes are part of growing up, part of life.*

Liz: What about other gynecological issues for large women?

Robin: *Yeast infections can be a problem, particularly for diabetics. Of course, thin women who eat a lot of chocolate can have them, too, or anybody on antibiotics.*

Liz: Any other concerns?

Robin: *Because we have more fat on our bodies, larger women have an abundance of estrogen. That can lead to irregular periods or breakthrough bleeding, and can increase the threat of cancer of the uterus. And, more fat in the diet can increase the risk of breast cancer.*

Liz: Sometimes larger people feel intimidated, even discriminated against, by the medical community. Is that our imagination?

Robin: *The truth is, it's easier to practice medicine on skinny people, logistically. Big people can be harder to examine. I have to be extra careful not to miss something. If, for example, I am not able to adequately feel a large woman's ovaries, I'll order an ultrasound, just to get a better reading. And, it can be more difficult to do surgery on a large person. These procedures certainly can be done, it just takes more time. Unfortunately, a woman who is self-conscious about her size may not go to her gynecologist for her annual pap smear and exam or seek out routine medical care, just because she's concerned about getting on the scale. Of course, I understand that fear.*

Liz: What is it like for you, being a big, beautiful woman doctor?

Robin: *In general, being beautifully abundant is like being a left-handed person living in a right-handed world. Actually, the only real problem with practicing medicine and being large is finding scrub suits that fit! I now carry my own scrubs with me and hoard them in my locker at the hospital. It would be terrible to miss a delivery just because I couldn't find scrub pants in my size! All of us larger docs and nurses hide our scrubs where we know we can find them when we need them, and I keep a couple in my car, just in case.*

Liz: Do you see any advantages to being large?

Robin: *When you are statuesque, it's a lot harder for people to ignore you. When you are able to look them in the eye and say, "I beg your pardon? Say that again?" they do listen. I guess our body language just talks louder! I hate to speak in public, but the few times I've done it, the response has been very positive. Maybe it's been my content more than my delivery, but I think the power and authority of my size has been an asset.*

Liz: Anything we haven't covered?

Robin: *I see a lot of patients who are growing older, women who are peri-menopausal and distressed about the changes in the body habitus: their upper arms have become heavier, their hips are larger, their tummy has gotten poochy, all because of hormonal changes. It's not that they've gained weight, just that it's been redistributed. This can be very traumatic for women of all sizes. These are natural changes, and part of maturity is dealing with these changes. The good news is, if body image is not such a crucial issue to you, these changes will not be that difficult to handle. Coming to terms with your body now can really help. Let's face it, "big" isn't politically correct and "old" isn't politically correct either. The real changes that need to take place will happen between the ears!*

"You Are What You Eat"
(If That Were True,
I'd Be Yogurt)

After we've worked through our self-esteem issues, dealt with our "old tapes" and learned to let go of the need to wear a size 6, there's yet another issue to deal with: eating. That time-consuming, mind-consuming experience we face three times a day or more, every day of our lives.

Let's Make Dinner

Consider how many steps go into preparing one simple meal, like Sunday dinner (the kind Mom used to make):

1. Plan what you're going to serve.
2. Browse through a few cookbooks for ideas. (Just the pictures make you hungry, so you nibble on some chips while you keep turning the pages. These do not count as real food.)
3. Check the refrigerator and shelves to see what you have on hand. (Vow to do something with the potatoes before they walk out of the pantry by themselves.)

4. Make a grocery list.
5. Go through your stack of coupons (most of which expired in 1985).
6. Find your car keys.
7. Drive to the local Piggly-Wiggly.
8. Spend a good forty-five minutes wandering aimlessly up and down the aisles, because you left your list on the kitchen table.
9. Spend another fifteen minutes at the checkout counter, while your frozen yogurt melts.
10. Haul the groceries out to the car. (One bag tears open while loading it into the backseat.)
11. Pull into your driveway, and drag in all the bags.
12. Put everything away while you toss a few cocktail peanuts in your mouth. The ones you bought for the candy dish—for company.
13. Wash the dishes in the sink, then scrape the crusty gray stuff off the cutting board.
14. Scrub all the fresh vegetables.
15. Make a salad: tear the lettuce, slice the tomatoes, grate the cheese, chop the bacon, cut the cucumber into cute little shapes, and pour on the dressing. Low-cal, not too much, and don't forget the croutons.

Tired yet? We haven't even made it to the main course! It's an amazing amount of work for one meal. We still have vegetables to prepare, meat to fix, biscuits to beat (remember I live in the South), and potatoes to wrestle, not to mention desserts (which is "stressed" spelled backwards!).

Women and the Food Thing

In addition to all the genetic and gender-specific reasons that women deal with the issue of gaining weight, maybe the fact that we're often the ones in charge of putting food on the table is a contributing factor.

My mom, bless her buxom heart, fed as many as six kids and one hubby three meals a day for over forty years. She scribbled a weekly menu on the back of a used envelope, then called in her grocery list to a local meat market that delivered her order in boxes right to our back door (Can you imagine? Now that's what I call convenience food!).

I was the typical spoiled baby of the family and did little more than put the food away for her. Mom did all the cooking and most of the dishes. Think how many hours of her day, of her life, were centered around feeding her family.

Is this a bad thing, a degrading job, a useless activity? Of course not! Every bookstore owner will tell you that their two perennial bestsellers are cookbooks and diet books. (The Bible still holds the #1 spot.)[1] Preparing a delicious meal is at least a specialized skill if not an art form, and the women and men among us who do it well are to be applauded.

In our household, Bill does as much cooking as I do, if not more. Must be a survival move. In truth, I think he actually enjoys cooking. I can take it or leave it (mostly, leave it). It's fun whipping something up for company, but night after night it gets old.

Nonetheless, the "mother is in charge of the kitchen" adage is still going strong in the 90's. If I call Bill at work just to say hello, he often asks me, "What's for dinner?" I, of course, haven't a clue and say so.

"Take some chicken out of the freezer," he suggests. A few hours later, chicken is on the table, thanks to hubby's helpful handiwork. (P.S. No, you can't have him!)

This example sure blows my "women gain weight because they do all the cooking" theory right out of the dishwater. Maybe preparing the food is not the issue. Maybe food itself — both eating and avoiding it — is the issue.

Sophia Loren said, "Everything you see I owe to spaghetti." (Oh, really? Then, why doesn't pasta with red sauce do that to me?)

Women have a thing about food, like men have a thing about sex. We think about it a lot, even fantasize about it. We feel righteous when we abstain, naughty when we enjoy something "forbidden."

I don't think I'm exaggerating when I say that women have a relationship with food. It is a friend and companion, or an enemy, a traitor. It has a powerful emotional component, especially since certain foods evoke strong memories from our childhood.

Food Memories

What foods have a memory link for you? I remember my Grandma Amidon's gingerbread cookies, cinnamon rolls and French bread. If I close my eyes, I can see her slight form at our red kitchen counter, bent over, stirring something wonderful in a yellow ceramic bowl. I can smell it, taste it, feel the flour on her hands, hear the pin rolling over the dough, watch her shaking the red and white can of cinnamon. It's an all-encompassing experience, arousing all my senses. When Pillsbury said, "Nuthin' says lovin' like somethin' from the oven," they knew exactly what they were talking about. Powerful memories, those.

Is it any wonder we turn to food when we're depressed, discouraged, disappointed, defeated? Food takes us back to a happier time, people and places we've loved, memories we cherish. No wonder they call it "comfort food!"

It doesn't have to be a negative emotion that opens the refrigerator door, though. Every celebration also includes food — every party, family occasion, baptism, graduation, wedding, anniversary. When I travel the country speaking at banquets and other special events, I confess to the audience that my whole job can be summed up in just two words: TALKING and EATING!

Those of us in the church really love to eat. Hey, if you can't smoke, drink, cuss, dance or fool around (and why would you want to?), then bring on the potluck dinner! My very first "Ladies Salad Supper" in the summer of '82 was a real eye-opener. Salad, my foot. Oh sure, there was a little lettuce around the edge of the bowl, but in the middle were marshmallows, sour cream, pretzels, jello, fruit, pecans, mayonnaise, whipped topping and who-knows-what-else. A little bit of heaven, right there in the fellowship hall.

Why Do We Eat?

"Well, why *do* I eat?" I've asked myself that many times over the years, and the complexity of the answer leaves me shaking my head. These are some of the reasons I've come up with:

Nourishment. Our bodies absolutely need food, demand food, would perish without it. That's why the methods that work for abstaining from alcohol, tobacco and drugs don't work for food. We can function without those substances. But we have been eating since pre-birth. That's why fasting, VLCD's (Very Low Calorie Diets) and any attempts to interfere with the body's nutritional needs will eventually backfire.

Habit. At 7:00 A.M., Noon and 6:00 P.M., something inside me goes "BONG!" (Sometimes, at 10:00 A.M. and 3:00 P.M., it also goes "ping!") This is not a bad thing, but it is clock-based rather than hunger-based. It is not as good a reason to eat (but then, sometimes, who needs a reason?). As Shakespeare wrote, "How use doth breed a habit in a man." (Or in a woman!)

Social Custom. Wherever I go, it seems food is served. It can be refused, of course, at the risk of offending the hostess. But gatherings and food go together. These are the occasions that feel dangerous to many of us who are trying to get off the diet treadmill. Social eating usually has little to do with real hunger.

Emotional Need. I once kept track on paper of what feelings I was experiencing while I was reaching for food. The answer was simple: all of them. Every emotion, from anger to anxiety, boredom to bereavement, celebration to cynicism. Even when I felt zealous, I reached for food! Do I have a right to do this? Yes. Is it the best thing for my body? Depends. Paul said, "All things are lawful for me, but all things are not helpful."[2]

Taste. I almost forgot this one. We might eat something just to see what it tastes like, or to experience the pleasure of it again. Taste buds like to have fun too! Like Erma Bombeck says, "I am not a glutton. I am an explorer of food."

Why Can't We Stop Eating?

I think the big question is: When is eating a pleasurable pursuit, and when is it compulsive? When you no longer enjoy eating, that's a good reason to stop and re-evaluate it. Not because you want to lose weight, or because you feel fat, or because you want to exert some "willpower." Forget those things. Focus on getting to know your body's needs better. Then you can respond honestly to real hunger versus emotional hunger, and eat because it is fun instead of eating food you don't even remember putting in your mouth. I don't think that eating compulsively is God's best choice for us. His Creation is filled with plants, fruits, vegetables, nuts, the fowl of the air, the fish of the sea, the beasts of the land, and they are primarily there for our nourishment and enjoyment. Period. These, then, are the two best reasons to eat: nourishment and enjoyment. Moliere was famous for saying, "One must eat to live, and not live to eat."

This may be where the fact that we are female comes into the picture. Men as a rule do not struggle with, "Shall I eat?" They eat because their stomach is growling, because it is lunchtime, because food is put in front of them, because it tastes good, because they enjoy eating. The same reasons that we eat, but without the heavy emotional undertones. Much less angst, much less "bad" and "good" foods, a whole lot less "what will this do to my hips?"

Men seldom sit around plotting what they will eat at their next meal, because they probably ate enough at their last meal to hold them a few hours. Women, on the other hand — ever dieting, ever measuring — are often obsessed with what they'll get to eat next *because they are always hungry!*

Talking Cells

Getting off the diet treadmill means taking better care of your body's needs, including feeding your hungry cells! First you have to figure out what they are hungry for. Cells don't talk. Or do they?

When I became pregnant with Matthew in 1986, one of the things I noticed immediately was my cravings. Never mind pickles and ice cream, I wanted green beans. Not dripping in butter or fatback, just fresh, steamed green beans. M-m-m-m. And oranges, mandarin oranges especially. I was good for two cans a day. We fully expected our firstborn to have orange-tinted skin and green ears!

A baby's tiny life has big needs, and God makes sure that we pay attention to them. Those cravings are real, and they are a good example of how our bodies talk to us. We tend to hear them more when we are pregnant because that is a time when we focus on what's happening to our bodies. We notice every subtle (and not so subtle!) change, as well as every movement in our abdomens. It's no wonder we also notice what we're really hungry for.

It's been several years since I carried a baby in my womb, but I still find if I slow down and pay attention, my appetite often leads me to particular preferences, and healthy ones to boot. Until we teach them otherwise, children have very intelligent appetites. Toddlers know when they are hungry, and it has nothing to do with the clock. When we say to them, "Not now, dear, supper is only an hour away," no wonder they start crying! They are hungry right then. My Lillian will say, "My tummy is empty," and that's exactly what she means. She knows when she's hungry and, most of the time, what she is hungry for—bananas, turkey or grapes. (And, sometimes, pizza!)

If our body starts craving complex carbohydrates, for example, we often interpret that as "I want cookies! I want cake!" That may be more sugar than our body was really looking for. When we eat it, it doesn't really satisfy that need. We eat more cookies, more cake, and may end up with that fuzzy-headed feeling, that cloudy sugar high, without ever making our body happy.

Next time your appetite says "cookies," just for fun, slip it something like a warm, delicious baked potato. I know what you're thinking: "I don't have time to bake a potato!" Plenty of fast food places have them, and the old microwave can zap you one in short order. Besides, talk about comfort food! My dear friend Evelyn craved potatoes so much she carried a picture of a big, fluffy baked potato in her wallet throughout her pregnancy. (Ev is a little different. That's why we get along!)

Am I saying don't eat the cookie? This is Liz speaking, your friend. By all means, if the cookie is what you really want, have it. Have several. But getting in tune with your body's nutritional needs should still be a priority for women of all sizes. Good health comes from many things you can't change (heredity and genetics) and a few things you can (nutrition and movement).

Games Dieters Play

If we're honest with ourselves, some of us are pretty adept at food games, especially in restaurants. We order fish ("it's better for me than beef"), but we order it fried. Or we order a chef's salad loaded with cheeses, meat and dressing, but say, "I only had a salad at lunch today!" Maybe we choose a light entree, then splurge on dessert, thinking it will all balance out somehow.

We may walk three blocks on the way to lunch and figure that such an effort should earn us an extra dinner roll or two. Or, we have carrot cake for dessert because that has to be good for us: after all, it's made out of carrots. (Please don't hear one word of condemnation in all this: I took these examples from my own life.)

I love the story of the woman who professed to be dieting, but had eight frozen cheesecakes in her freezer. Her explanation was simple: "They were on sale."[3] Then there's the hostess who kept a candy dish symmetrical by reducing the M & M's to the same number of each color. Or how about the teenager who drinks a diet soda while eating a candy bar?

Get serious. Diet foods are a joke. As one woman said: "Diet foods? I mean, really! Hawaiian Punch Lite?!"

The time has come to stop playing games and be more honest with our eating. By focusing on nutrition and enjoyment, instead of calories and pounds, the experience becomes one of common sense rather than compulsion, of honest emotions rather than stuffed feelings.

No More Games

Here is an outrageous idea: fill your house with healthy foods. Pack the refrigerator with fresh fruits. Keep the crisper filled with veggies, and stock the shelves with whole grains, legumes and pasta. Replace your soda cans with fruit juices, toss some frozen yogurt in the freezer, along with chicken breasts and fish. And, yes, go ahead and throw in some Twinkies, nacho chips, or whatever rings your bell. The things you really do crave on occasion. Then eat what you need, when you need it.

Oh, my stars! I will gain two hundred pounds!

Really? Ever tried it? Spontaneously eating healthy foods is the best thing you can do for your body. Sure, sometimes you'll reach for the stuff with a little less nutritional value. But so what? Everybody does that. Thin people, healthy people, old people, young people. Everybody eats potato chips and nobody has died from them yet.

David Garner, Ph.D. is the director of research at the Eating Disorders Section, Department of Psychiatry at Michigan State University. His advice? "Stop dieting. This means start eating regular meals, including appropriate sweets and snacks. Many people who have struggled for years find that when they give up dieting they do not gain weight."[4]

What's an "appropriate" sweet or snack? Well, it's your body: ask it! When you're hungry, have some healthy choices available for the nutrients they provide, and give your body the fuel it needs to function. (When only a cupcake will make you happy, that's what you should eat, guilt-free.)

Whatever you do, enjoy what you eat! If you are not hungry for carrots, for heaven's sake, don't force them between your lips. One woman said dieting conjured up, "ugly, ugly thoughts of carrot sticks pounded into my heart like a stake."

Transylvania time! Restricted eating, better known as dieting, gets us primed for the day we'll go off that diet and binge on whatever foods we deprived ourselves of. Don't be deceived. The body will not be mocked. This divinely designed machine needs fuel at regular intervals in sufficient amounts. It will run best on the high octane stuff, but is so remarkable a contraption that it will run on almost anything. For a while. Dieting is like driving on fumes. It's hard on the engine. You could run out of gas at any moment. The smart driver keeps her tank filled and her engine tuned up, and she heads out for a spin regularly, just to keep her gears oiled. And, remember: the big Cadillac looks just as sharp on the open road as the little Honda!

3,500 Calories = One Pound

We've all been brainwashed into thinking that by just cutting our calorie intake by 500 calories a day, 3,500 calories a week, we will effortlessly lose one pound a week. Simple arithmetic, right?

That would be fine if we all processed those 500 calories in the same way, but we don't! Our metabolic rates can vary widely. For some folks, 1,500 calories a day would be a strict diet and they'd lose two pounds a week. For the next person, it would only mean one pound of weight loss. Some folks might not lose anything; others could *gain* weight on those same 1,500 calories a day.

On a recent plane trip to Texas, I watched as the flight attendants placed the exact same meal in front of all the passengers. (Maybe "meal" isn't the right word for it; "hot items" and "cold items" would fit better!)

As we all ate these identical foods in almost identical portion sizes, it struck me how differently our individual bodies were going to process that meal. We are not empty jars into which food is poured — just pour in less and there'll be less volume. Instead, we are incredible machines, very complex, each unique. God designed us to be different. And (I'll say it again) different is good!

Often in diet groups I attended, we were told that we would just have to accept the fact that some people could eat more than we did and not gain weight. Resign yourself to a life of reduced calories, they said, because your body needs fewer calories. What if, instead, we accept the fact that our bodies were meant to be, designed to be, bigger! We need healthy foods in healthy amounts. We will never wear a size 6 dress, but could wear a size 16 and be our healthiest, happiest self. Wouldn't that make more sense than semi-starving ourselves, beating ourselves up for not being thinner, and making ourselves and our families miserable? Of course.

Here's a novel thought: when we are dieting, we feel in control of our eating. In reality, we're obsessed with our eating, or non-eating. It's all we think about or plan for. Our lives revolve around it. How many times have you said, "I'll diet when I'm ready" or "I'll diet when the time is right." Exactly. Dieting takes so much effort that it is all you could conceivably do. That is not reality, and not a life worthy of pursuit.

When we put food in the proper perspective—a source of nutrition, energy and enjoyment—that's when we're really in control. Our emotional selves do need nurturing, but not with food! In her terrific book, *Inner Eating*, Shirley Billigmeier states:

> By struggling, withholding food, and putting yourself on restrictive diets, you make life more difficult for yourself. If you separate the two issues (emotions and body care), you can learn to handle both better.[5]

We all have seen examples of thin people who are not in the least bit healthy, who eat all the wrong foods, never exercise, and so forth.

Most of my friends are "small" and in terrible health. Gallbladder, arthritis, diabetes, and so on. Is it possible to be overweight and healthy?

Elaine from Ohio

It's time to say this again: if you are a large woman, you may not be overeating at all. Your eating may not be emotionally based in the least. All of us have different *everything*—metabolic rates, nutritional needs, fat-to-muscle ratios, everything. Relax. My only encouragement to you is to seek honest eating.

One of my college dormitory mates told me that she would never understand why I was overweight. After a few months of living in the same building, she noticed that I rarely snacked or over-indulged. She could not understand this and even asked me if I was a "closet" eater, which I am happy to say I am not. It gave me a better sense of what I was up against.

Mary Ann from New York

Mary Ann found out what many of us have suspected: we do indeed eat normally, we aren't the gluttons we think we are. After all, the word "glutton" means, "one who eats excessively." It comes from a word meaning "to gulp" and has only to do with eating, nothing to do with body size.[6]

In *Making Peace with Food*, author Susan Kano suggests we "enjoy eating, avoid being fanatical or rigid about the choices you make, eat in harmony with your hunger and satiation, and try to keep dieters' mind-set from creeping into your efforts."[7]

Eat in peace, free from games, denial, apology, worry. That stuff weighs a ton! Your body can be trusted today, as is, right now, this minute. Treat it with respect, and watch what happens!

Begin Building Body Confidence Today

1. Start listening to your body for clear directives. What are you really hungry for? Begin keeping your refrigerator and shelves stocked with those items.

2. Whenever your body says, "I am hungry!" give it water first. We need lots of it, and you may just be thirsty. Still hungry? By all means, eat what you are hungry for.

3. Stop comparing notes with others, and eat what makes *you* feel good and function well. Above all, stop dieting!

❤ A Nutritionist Speaks . . .

Dr. Kayla Carruth received her Ph.D. in nutrition from the University of Tennessee. She is now director of program development for health education at the University of Tennessee Medical Center in Knoxville.

Liz: Why are American women getting bigger?

Kayla: *Actually, the whole population is getting bigger! In general, it's fair to say that part of the growth in our body size is that women are beginning to feel freer to be themselves, rather than follow the trends that fashion sets for us.*

Liz: In part, then, it's a social movement. What else?

Kayla: *Once we hit around forty, our muscle mass starts declining. For men, this doesn't happen till about age fifty. So, we have to do something proactive to even maintain muscle, let alone increase the muscle mass. When fat replaces muscle, less energy is used to process the nutrients coming into the cells, and the metabolic rate will lower further.*

Liz: So age enters into the picture. Other factors?

Kayla: *Genetic predisposition plays a big part. When it comes to health, it pays to choose your parents well. I always tell patients to look at their family tree, in particular their mother, sisters, grandmother, and aunts. (Of course, some of us take after the male side of the family tree too.) If everybody in your family is tall, big boned and heavy, you are probably going to be the same way, unless you were adopted.*

Liz: If we are genetically programmed to be larger, why are some of us so unhappy with our bodies?

Kayla: *Our expectations of our bodies have not been very realistic. Social pressures are so great, especially for younger women, many of whom haven't yet established their own identity.*

Liz: Do diets work?

Kayla: *Theoretically, you can lose weight on any diet. But unless you truly change your life style habits through behavior modification, you will indeed gain it back. And changing those habits is very difficult because you developed your current eating pattern — what you eat, how much and how often — over dozens of years.*

Liz: What changes could be made, then?

Kayla: *Forget dieting! Eat healthy foods and really work on the other life style habits, things that make you active. Lower your fat intake significantly and eat a wide variety of foods. Think of this as change for a healthier body, not as punishment. Never go below 1,200 calories a day. Making time for regular exercise each day is equally important.*

Liz: At 4'11", you are a petite woman. How is size an issue for you?

Kayla: *"One size doesn't fit" all for me either! I would say 90-95% of the time I am not aware of being smaller. Only when someone points it out to me am I aware of it.*

Liz: Do any situations like that come to mind?

Kayla: *I can remember walking through an airport and being stared at so intently by a woman that I thought perhaps I knew her, so I spoke to her. She came back with a question: "How tall are you?" When I told her, she explained, "I saw you and said to my husband, 'Look how short that woman is!' and he said I was the same size, and I told him, 'No way!' So, I just had to find out how short you really were."*

Liz: Good grief!

Kayla: *I was angry. I guess it never occurred to her that her story might hurt my feelings. I'm glad my husband was with me. Marrying someone six feet tall has been a big help, because he sees me as being just as tall as he is!*

"All Fat People Are Lazy"

The year was 1978. I was twenty-four years old, 171 pounds. A solid size 14 — a 12, if there was elastic in the waist. I'd signed up for a jazz dance class with an instructor everyone raved about. I loved to dance, always had. From my toddler days when my older sisters taught me how to do the "Twist" at their slumber parties, I loved the way my body felt when it moved across a polished wooden floor, music pounding in the background. I could hardly wait for that first dance class. I wore the standard black leotard and tights (workout gear was not as slinky and colorful in those days), and the black soft ballet slipper. Plunking down my money, I signed my name to the day's roster and stepped into the dance studio.

Mirrors were everywhere. Sunlight poured through the windows, and the wood beneath my feet felt warm. The music began. Rhythmic, energetic, magnetic. My body responded instinctively. Swaying, stretching, bending. Oh, it felt wonderful to move to music again!

I stayed in the back row with the other beginners, carefully watching the women in front, mimicking their every move. One, two, step, step, lunge, back, slide, slide. I'm a quick study and soon could feel my pulse pick up at the excitement of moving again, doing something so right, so good for my body and myself. Then it happened. My eyes caught the instructor following my every move, and she was smirking. No, make that laughing. I looked around. Had

I missed something amusing? I turned back to her with a quizzical look on my face, and she put words to my fears: "You look so funny when you move!" The rest of the class giggled and kept dancing.

That was it. I finished class that day, but I never went back. Not to that class, not to any class until 1982, the year I starved myself down to 155 (for about a week), and joined an aerobics class. The instructor was a friend, and would never have dared say anything more challenging to me than, "Go for the burn!" (That was the big deal in those days, along with "No pain, no gain." Oh brother.)

When the Music Stops

I stopped dancing in those "lost" years, even in the privacy of my own home. (Who was going to see me there? The UPS guy?) Instead, I told people that I had four very effective means of exercise:

1. Jogging my memory
2. Climbing the walls
3. Jumping to conclusions
4. Throwing my weight around

Funny, yes, but sad too. I'd taken one insensitive instructor's pronouncement that I looked silly when I danced, and made it my prison.

In their excellent book, *Great Shape*, Pat Lyons and Debby Burgard state, "this fear of wondering what others will think. . . probably keeps more large women inactive than any other factor, even the fear of injury. It is as if splitting our pants or having someone laugh at us would be more painful than breaking a leg."[1]

It does seem foolish to be fearful of a sideways glance, a giggle or the "rrrr-rip" of a pant seam. But that fear is real for many of us, and not to be discounted. It does not, however, have to be endured; it can be faced and overcome.

When the 1982 diet dissolved into the 1984 gain, I knew I'd never diet again, with a capital D. I was, however, ready to dance! I called all around town until I found a woman willing to give me private lessons at a reasonable price. Out came the black leotards once more (in a larger size, of course).

But no ballet slippers this time. No, something a little noisier, something that fit my ever-growing level of confidence, something that always makes people smile: tap dancing shoes!

A Real Toe-Tapper

Ada Lee is the queen of tap in our town, a veteran teacher of hundreds of second graders slugging their way through "Shuffle One, Shuffle Two." She did not laugh at me. In fact, she told me after our first lesson that if I was willing to work hard and practice, I could be one swell tap dancer.

Well, I tapped all right. All 195 pounds of me worked out on a little patch of wooden floor in my Oak Street cottage. I took my tap shoes into the radio station and tapped live, on the air. When I met Bill in 1985, I greeted him at the door "en tappe," and blew him away. In short, I had a great time and gave my cardiovascular system a dandy workout as well, because tap dancing *is* serious exercise.

When the babies came and my feet swelled, the size 8 1/2 tap shoes were put away for good. But not my spiral notebook with Ada Lee's careful diagrams and instructions. No, that notebook is waiting for a new pair of size 10 tap shoes to show up in my closet!

Maybe this is a novel concept to you: exercise for fun? Not to lose weight? Not to burn calories? Just to. . . enjoy it? Absolutely. Adriane Fugh-Berman, M.D., board member of the National Women's Health Network, said: "Exercise is as good for your mind as it is for your body — it can lessen depression, anxiety, and insomnia, and is a good all-purpose stress reliever."[2] Not a word there about losing weight, but plenty about good health.

Good for Every Body

Unfortunately, for many of us movement and exercise are deemed valuable for one purpose only: to get some extra pounds off. In addition to those crazy calorie charts we've all memorized, I also spent some early years studying how many calories I'd burn while, say, riding my bike. It was very discouraging. A whole hour biking only burns 175 calories? Good heavens, why bother? Let's have an ice cream cone instead.

What the charts didn't say was, the cardiovascular benefits of biking continue long after the bike is back in the garage. Building muscle mass also contributes to a higher metabolic rate. As Dr. Fugh-Berman notes, "A pound of muscle needs 30 to 50 calories a day just for maintenance, while fat only needs two calories a day to get along."[3]

In *Great Shape*, the authors point out the negative side effects of dieting: "slowed metabolic rate, sluggishness, loss of muscle mass, feelings of deprivation." These are just the opposite of the benefits of exercise: "heightened metabolic rate, increased energy, increased muscle mass — and feelings of well-being."[4] The obvious conclusion: don't diet, exercise!

Recently, after several months of being too busy to exercise (sound familiar?), I jumped up and went for a long walk. Here's what I wrote in my journal when I got home:

> That was one of the most positive experiences I've had all week. It felt good, like coming out of my shell. I saw a neighbor and she smiled. I tried to smile back. My calves started hurting about half way around the block, but that's okay. I did it!

Every time I've ever done something that would qualify as exercise, I've been glad I did it. There may have been times I've regretted (rightly or wrongly) what I ate, but I've never been sorry I exercised! Guilt or regret is never the by-product of movement (unless we try to do too much too soon, and are injured. Be good to yourself and go s - l - o - w.).

If you find yourself dragging at the end of the day, believe it or not, you need *more* movement, not less.

Walk, Don't Run

Walking is my favorite exercise for many valid reasons:

1. I don't need any special equipment, just my feet (which, to be sure, are very special size 10 equipment!).
2. I can walk anywhere, anytime, without planning ahead or making an appointment.
3. It's free!
4. It requires little concentration, so I can take in my surroundings or let my imagination soar.
5. I may break into a sweat, but it usually doesn't mess up my hair. So I can walk whenever the mood strikes, even if I have an important appointment later that day.
6. Walking requires absolutely NO squat-thrusts!

If you diet *without* exercise, you hit your body with a double whammy, and your metabolic rate undoubtedly takes a dive. Not good. If you diet *with* exercise, you'll probably see some good results (mostly from the exercise), and now you'll want to increase your food intake and have more energy. If you exercise without *dieting*, then you're right on target as far as your metabolic rate is concerned.

Your basal metabolic rate, the calories your body burns at rest, accounts for most of your daily calories expenditure. In other words, if you stayed in bed all day and didn't lift a finger, you'd still burn about 70% of your normal daily calories. (I don't recommend this, but wanted you to know how your body works.) Another 10% of calories are burned just digesting and absorbing the foods you've eaten. That leaves 20% of your caloric intake to be burned off with exercise.[5]

The conclusion? Stop thinking about food and start thinking about movement. Is it possible to become too compulsive about exercise? Of course. Since the fitness craze hit in the 70's, we could all probably name someone whose over-commitment to exercise got out of hand. One fitness expert said, "I've begun to worry that the fitness revolution has brought us just a new way to strive for the same unreasonable goals."[6]

Personally, I'm not too worried about developing an obsession with exercise. I try to sneak in a little movement where I can, avoiding the "E" word ("exercise") because it brings back grim memories of gym.

P.E. Stands for Painful Experience

I don't know if it was my instructor — short hair, no makeup, big calves, loud bark — or me, but I dreaded gym for six years running. I'd have graduated with a much higher grade point average, but because of all those C's in P.E. I came in twentieth in a class of two hundred.

Maybe it was that powder blue gym uniform, designed by someone who'd never played hockey while wearing a short dress with a full circle skirt and bloomers underneath. BLOOMERS! With "Liz" stitched on the right cheek. Oh, please.

In team sports I was, as you might expect, the last one chosen for the team. Even my closest friends picked me last, then said, "I'm sorry, but we want to win!" The only exception was basketball, a sport where my 5'9" body was worth something. I played a lot of Saturday ball at the playground, shot baskets after school, and tried out for the junior varsity team in 9th grade. When I made the first cut, I was so happy I cried all the way home. I didn't make the second cut, but that was okay. My body had served me well and done its best.

I tried out for hockey too, but never made it past day one of tryouts. In retrospect, I'm so proud of myself for even trying. The tenacity and courage I developed throughout my teen years has served me well on the playing field of life.

Since most of my friends were cheerleaders (I think they liked to keep me around for comic relief), it was only natural that I'd try out for cheerleading. I knew every cheer, every jump, could do a mean split and by the third year of tryouts, could turn a decent cartwheel.

The cheerleading coach was also my English teacher, which happened to be my best subject. I knew she'd give me a fair shot. It was my freshman year of high school, my third year to try out and, I had decided, my last. The rejection was beginning to take its toll.

I practiced until I had spider veins in my thighs from clapping and slapping. Even my Dad knew all the cheers by heart. My cartwheel was awesome, all legs in motion. I was in great shape, great voice, a 140-pound wonder, the all-American blonde, and I was ready.

Three days of practice, then the main event. White blouse, blue shorts, white socks, saddle shoes. Thankfully, it was a good hair day.

When my name was called, I moved to the center of the gym with confidence and performed my routine with gusto. I can still hear Coach Sally's comment when I finished: "Great voice!"

The kiss of death. Great voices do not great cheerleaders make. Face it, Liz, you just didn't look the part. You were simply too much woman for the job. (I've since read that cheerleaders often ruin their voices for life, and develop a permanent raspiness from too much shouting in their formative years. God must have spared my voice for radio and platform speaking. For that, I'm grateful.)

One interesting point: I dieted and exercised constantly at that time, and still the scale stayed at 140 pounds and wouldn't budge. I was unquestionably fit, but not model-thin, because my body was not built to be a size 6 model! Unfortunately, what I did to my metabolism at age fourteen wasn't smart, healthy, or in tune with my body's needs.

Learning to Move Again

That was then, this is now. We cannot change the past, but we definitely can impact the present. Now, we are no longer given a grade for our exercise efforts (or if we are, it's always an A for attempt!), nor do we have a whole panel of judges watching us when we work out. One of the many joys of adulthood is not having to measure up to anyone's standard of fitness but our own. I think for most of us, the real stumbling block is time. Have you ever found yourself saying, "I'd love to exercise if I just had more time?" That was always my constant refrain. Now, I have a new one: "Can I walk right now? Can I stretch and bend, right here, for five minutes?" The answer is almost always, "Yes, I can!" And so I do. It feels terrific. Will I burn calories, will I lose weight? Good heavens, who cares? Will it improve my muscle tone, circulation, and flexibility? Yes indeed, and make me feel better to boot. That's enough.

Here's another change I'm learning to make. With two young children still eager to please their mother (I know, these days are numbered), it's easy to say to them, "Would you bring Mommy her coat? Would you take this to Daddy?" instead of getting up and doing it myself. On other occasions I've witnessed Bill sprawled across the staircase because he tripped over a pile of things I left on the bottom step for my "next trip up." I'm also notorious for driving around and around a parking lot, looking for the space nearest the door. On a rainy day that's understandable, but on a beautiful sunny day it's unnecessary.

These are the "time savers" I'm learning to undo.

Do I agree with the fable, "All fat people are lazy?" No way! Some of us are so industrious we border on workaholism. The last thing we are is lazy. I do find a pattern in my own life, though, of looking for physical shortcuts and avoiding exertion. It's just habit, not a character flaw, and I am moving toward more movement every day.

In *Making Peace with Food* Susan Kano offers goals for any exercise program, including some we've already talked about: having fun, feeling better and improving health. She also sees exercise as a great way to "promote a less ornamental and more instrumental body view" and to "develop unconditional body acceptance and appreciation."[7] Although a small woman herself, Susan is an advocate for body confidence at any size. Bless her!

From the Publishers of "Lose Weight While You Sleep" . . .

A booklet called *Instant Fitness* caught my eye while I stood in line at the grocery store recently. It was displayed among a whole series of booklets with equally outrageous titles: *Birth Signs to Improve Your Love Life*, *150 Beauty Tricks of TV Stars* and *Know Your Lucky Numbers*. Oh sure.

The back cover of this book declared, "It's fun and it's easy to own a well-proportioned figure! Re-shape yourself into a stunning new body that will have heads turning and make you feel like a new woman!" I knew it was worth the seventy-five cent investment, just for the laughs.

I was not disappointed. The first chapter was "How to Flatten Your Stomach." Their advice was to "try to keep your stomach muscles pulled in at all times." The next chapter was "How to Flatten Your Thighs." (Of all the things in life I've ever yearned for, *flat thighs* are not one of them.) They suggested cutting down on salt intake to achieve the desired results.

The chapter titled "Firm Up Flabby Areas" warned against staying in one position too long, which can cause "molecular stagnation." Horrors. In a section on "Mental Conditioning," the reader is told to "Think about how charming you will be with a slim new figure. Think about the new winning personality that will go with that figure." I guess that means at present, the reader is neither charming nor personable.

The final pages contain this sage advice: "Don't be disappointed if some of your friends fail to praise you for making your figure trim. Some people are hostile to those who successfully lose weight — because they can't do it themselves." Oh, brother!

All this would be good clean fun if it weren't taken so seriously by the hundreds of women who purchase such guides every week. Even the title is a fable: "Instant Fitness." There is nothing instant about getting fit. And fitness does not rule out fatness. Despite Covert Bailey's insistence that we are either "fit or fat," it's not impossible to be both at the same time.

In an article titled, "Fat and Fit: An Idea Whose Time Has Come," fitness expert and author Pat Lyons, R.N., M.A., states that "regular exercise has been shown to have wonderful health benefits, regardless of whether weight is lost. Exercise is also a prime component in stabilizing weight, a legitimate health goal because it places far less stress on the body than constant fluctuations do."[8]

One of the participants in her "Great Shape" exercise program summed up this approach perfectly: "I feel healthier now than any diet I was ever on, and everyone in class has improved health-wise. And we all smile and enjoy life more."[9]

Exercising for the sole purpose of losing weight tends to be (like dieting) short-term, ineffective and self-defeating. Putting movement in your life to improve health and well-being, and for sheer enjoyment, tends to be (unlike dieting) long-term. Plus, it effectively lowers blood pressure and reduces the need for insulin in some diabetics.

Fitness Fears

The truth is, even with all those healthy benefits, many of us are none too eager to jump into a fitness or sports program. It has nothing to do with laziness. One of our survey questions asked, "Does your size affect your social life?" Several women commented specifically about physical activity.

I'm afraid if I ski, I might fall and then couldn't get up.
Joann from Michigan

(This reminds me of the TV ad featuring the elderly woman moaning, "I've fallen and I can't get up!") Of course, many of us can identify with her honest fear. The solution? If she really wants to ski, she might take a friend who will be happy to help her get up! Or, she might find another winter sport that would be more fun and less frightening for her. Such fears are legitimate, just because they are hers. Only she can choose how to address them.

I used to be very athletic — now I've given up softball because my legs hurt when I play and I'm embarrassed to run — my stomach bounces. I would probably use our neighborhood swim and tennis club if I were smaller. I like to dance — now I become winded easier.
Joyce from Virginia

It's always easy to offer advice, isn't it? We might be quick to suggest that Joyce do more warm-up exercises so her legs won't hurt, or we might tell her to accept the fact that her windedness may come from age as much as weight. It's easy for us to say, "Put on your bathing suit and hit that swim club!" or "Who cares if your stomach bounces when you run?"

It's obvious that Joyce cares. We women of all sizes need to do less finger-wagging at one another and more hand-holding. If we try some of these activities together, maybe with a woman of our own size and at our level of fitness, the whole thing would become less scary.

Fitness Fashions

Some of us aren't hesitant about sports, dance or exercise because of the movement required, but because of the clothing issue.

I don't like to participate in activities that are real physical or require less clothing. (I mean, if I stuffed this body into a bathing suit I would clear the pool.)

Rosanna from Kentucky

Those darn bathing suits. We're talking about an article of clothing that dominates three entire months of the year, for heaven's sake. How many times has a magazine cover shouted at us, "Get Ready for Swimsuit Season!" It's never "Get Ready for Blue Jean Season" or "Leather Belt Season," but sure enough, June, July and August are "Bathing Suit Season" with a vengeance. Fat women need not apply.

Bathing suits conceal nothing, reveal everything. (They may be "suits," but very few have pockets!) One tabloid collection of the latest in swimwear fashion featured a suit with "adjustable triangles." (What a nice choice for a geometry major!) Those, of course, are not "one size fits all" triangles. (Is that an isosceles triangle or scalene? Obtuse or acute?)

I remember well my first two-piece bathing suit. It was yellow and white gingham check, very conservative, more like large squares than tiny triangles. It had a little modesty panel attached to the top with Velcro, and draped down to the pant leg. Great for covering tummy flab. I was twelve.

One year, I found a great two-piece suit that fit nicely but had, alas, no modesty panel. To make up for the missing panel, I arrived at the public swimming pool with a big beach towel tied around my waist. With practice, I learned to whip off the towel, spread it flat on the grass and lie down on it in one brief sweeping motion, executed with such speed that no one saw The Roll. If someone came by to speak to me, I didn't dare sit up. Instead I flipped over on my stomach and propped my head in my hands to talk while I tanned.

Actually, bathing suits have little to do with exercise, or even swimming, and everything to do with body image. It's not surprising the Miss America pageant features a swimsuit competition, because that's exactly what every American woman faces when she hits the beach: competition.

I say, skip the silly suit, wear shorts and a top or whatever's comfortable, and cavort in the waves all you like. It's truly a mind-over-matter issue: if you don't mind, it won't matter! Enjoy the splash of cool ocean water on your legs. Feel the warm, wet sand squish between your toes, and catch the scent of sea water while you romp on the shoreline. The activity is more important than how you look doing it.

For the local pool or swim club, practical one-piece suits are easily available from catalogues in sizes up to 26. Larger sizes can be custom-made. If swimming is the exercise your body craves, don't disappoint it by "waiting until you're thinner." As the athletic shoe people are fond of saying, "Just do it!"

Body Confidence in Action

Some women are elated to discover when push comes to shove, they do just fine in the exercise department. I love this story from a Virginia woman who found out her body functioned admirably when put to the test by her employer at an outdoor team building session. She and her coworkers had to climb a twenty-foot pole, scale a forty-foot wall and slide down a zip line from a forty-foot pole. Here's what happened:

> *My group of seven ladies who are desk-bound and only walk occasionally for exercise, was with a group of six guys from the shipping area who all work out during lunch at our on-site fitness center. All of us made it, and the guys didn't! We gained new respect.*
>
> Janet from Virginia

Congratulations, Janet and company! There's no doubt physical achievement of any kind, whether it's receiving a trophy for "Most

Improved Bowler" or making it to the top of the steps without getting winded, is an accomplishment worthy of applause. You may have to do all the clapping, but so be it!

No one can do it for you, and no one can take away what you have achieved. Mark Twain put it this way: "Skill and confidence are an unconquered army." Just as education gives you power, an advantage that can't be seen but can be experienced, physical exercise can give you a sense of wellness and body confidence. This may or may not be reflected in firmer muscles, but it's surely reflected in your smiling, confident face!

Professional Help

Speaking of education, you need to know about the Aerobics and Fitness Association of America (AFAA), a professional organization that boasts 50,000 members in seventy-three countries, and calls itself "the world's largest fitness educator." They conduct certification classes all the time, all over the country. One of the courses they offer is a special workshop called "Teaching the Overweight." Now, I love the concept of fitness classes just for us, but I *hate* the name. I called the AFAA toll-free line to tell them so. The woman who assisted me was most sympathetic, and very helpful. This special "Teaching the Overweight" certification can be earned only after an instructor earns the AFAA's Primary Certification. It's exciting to think there are fitness professionals all over America who've invested in our health and well-being by learning how to teach us safely and effectively.

I asked her, "How would I find such an instructor?" She recommended putting a small ad in the newspaper — "I am looking for an AFAA-certified instructor to lead a class for large women" — or post a similar notice on bulletin boards at local fitness centers. She assured me the phone would ring off the hook.

Having found an instructor, she suggested they might know of a class for larger women already underway in my city. The second option, she said, is to organize such a class myself, and advertise it.

The third option might be to find two or three friends and have our own class. The helpful woman from AFAA said the average hourly fee for such group instruction would be $15-$35 an hour, depending on your area of the country. The obvious appeal of these classes is two-fold: safe exercise and zero intimidation!

The Last Word on Moving Your Muscles

Fat people are by no means "lazy." Whether you choose to exercise or not, the decision is yours and should bear no weight of moral consequence.

You're not "bad" if you don't, or "good" if you do add movement to your life. Paul wrote Timothy that "bodily exercise profits a little, but godliness is profitable for all things."[10] Yes, exercise is good for your body, but it doesn't make you a good person. It might make you feel better, it might improve your health, and both are valid. But exercise should never be confused with moral or spiritual goodness. After all, you won't find the word "fitness," as we define it, in the Bible!

When it comes to the body (what the Greeks called "soma"), we can both overestimate and underestimate its value. To pay no heed to our bodies whatsoever is foolish and invites disaster. Sleep, food, water, shelter and moderate exercise are all necessary requirements for life on this planet.

But the Western world has gone overboard in its pursuit of the consummate healthy body; measuring foods by the ounce, fat composition by percentage and bodies by the pound. To our culture's way of thinking, less is always better. Paul asked the Colossians, "Why, as though living in the world, do you subject yourselves to regulations — 'Do not touch, do not taste, do not handle,' which all concern things which perish with the using — according to the commandments and doctrines of men?"[11] (Sure sounds like dieting to me!) Paul even declares, "Let no one judge you in food or in drink."[12] Of course, Paul was talking about the many food regulations that the religious types of his time loved to impose on one another. (Then again, for many folks today, being fit and trim *is* a religion, so maybe the analogy works better than one might think!)

We have only so many hours in each day. Assume for the moment you spend eight hours at work, seven hours sleeping, one hour driving, one hour bathing and dressing, one hour on household chores, one hour on the phone, and one hour watching television. That leaves four hours in your busy day. Do you want to spend them shopping, chopping, weighing, measuring, planning, preparing and agonizing over every morsel that goes in your mouth? Or do you want to spend that time stretching your muscles while you enjoy your favorite fun activity? Thirty minutes would be plenty. Less is okay too. Try ten minutes. Five minutes. Just begin.

Maybe you want to spend time with your family, or do something meaningful for the less fortunate around you. Whatever you do, seek out that which tastes like eternity and feels like forever. Like Ziggy says, "The waist is a terrible thing to mind."

Begin Building Body Confidence Today

1. Find a form of movement you can do right where you are, for 10 minutes. Anything counts: arm circles, marching in place, touching your toes. Do it now, for ten full minutes by the clock. (I just tried it and I feel wonderful! How do you feel?)

2. Find a form of movement that is *fun*, perhaps done with a group: a walking club, a dance class, a bowling league. Call about it. Ask them to send you some information.

3. Buy yourself one special item to encourage you: a new pair of sweats, a head band, new shoes, a snazzy leotard, a bathing suit. Make sure it fits now, not a size smaller for "when." Let it be your uniform for having fun!

❤ *A Fitness Expert Speaks. . . .*

Pat Lyons, R.N., M.A., is the regional health education consultant for Northern California Kaiser Permanente, the oldest and largest HMO in the world. Her background is in sports psychology and women's health, and her favorite sports include tennis, softball, skiing, ice skating and hiking. Pat is the co-author of *GREAT SHAPE: The First Fitness Guide for Large Women.*

Liz: Why do women of all sizes, but especially larger women, need to embrace exercise?

Pat: *It's a fundamental way for women to "come home" to their bodies. Sport, dance and movement help you trust your body again. We have a right to feel good, to enjoy physical strength and well-being.*

Liz: And your focus with *GREAT SHAPE* is on enjoyment, not losing weight, is that right?

Pat: *Yes! We need to stop seeing physical activity as punishment, and a thinner body as the only viable product of exercise. Not true! Being physically active is a way to nourish ourselves.*

Liz: We all know, theoretically, that exercise is good for us. Why don't we do it?

Pat: *The number one reason is, "I don't have enough time." The number two reason is, "I'm too embarrassed to go to a gym or exercise class. People make fun of me."*

Liz: Where do we, the great un-exercised, begin?

Pat: *It's a process of small steps. Find something you enjoy, that feels good to do, that's fun. Maybe something you did as a child, or a sport you played in school. Be creative! Your movement does not have to be an organized aerobics class. It could be square dancing or folk dancing.*

Liz: Or tap dancing!

Pat: *Right! Try different kinds of things, experiment, make enjoyment a priority. Get a buddy. Help each other, be easy on one other. Stay in the moment of the activity. Don't think about, "How much will I lose?" or any of that. Think about how much you are enjoying it. If you are out for a walk, smell the roses along the way!*

Liz: What if a woman says, "I'm too out of shape and too intimidated by group exercise things. I just can't do it."

Pat: *I understand that. The larger woman can't just "slip into" an exercise class unnoticed. And often, she can't keep up with the accelerated pace of a standard aerobics or step aerobics program. Start with climbing the stairs inside your own home. Dance around to your favorite music in the privacy of your living room. It takes a long time to change old habits, so relax. Break it down into really small pieces, and validate every small thing you do. Above all, do not focus on the weight loss benefits, which may be minimal, but rather on the health benefits, which are tremendous.*

Liz: Tell us more about that.

Pat: *Researchers from Stanford University found that exercising ten minutes at a time, three times a day is just as effective for improving health as exercising thirty minutes all at once.*

Liz: Hooray! That takes care of the "we don't have time" problem.

Pat: *Right. Their study was particularly aimed at determining health benefits for those with hypertension and diabetes. And the benefits of exercise are realized most by the people who are most sedentary. Every little effort for the sedentary person is really worthwhile. When it comes to exercise, let go of the results and get into the process. Fitness and health are for everybody. Let's enjoy it!*

"Things Would Be Perfect If I Were a Size 10"

Helen Hunt, who knew a lot about money, said, "There is a myth that if you amass enough wealth, then your life falls into place." Many people I've met over the years would buy into that "money equals happiness" fable, even though our newspapers are filled with stories of how wealth has ruined marriages, torn apart families to the third generation, and made hordes of people nigh unto miserable.

The same thing is true with body size. Lizzie's version is: "There is a myth that if you lose enough weight, then your life falls into place."

People buy into that, too, with every dime in their wallets. Roberta Pollack Seid writes in her book, *Never Too Thin*, that "the quest for a fit, fat-free body . . . is held in almost as much esteem as that older American ideal, making money."[1]

The title of this chapter is one of the most carefully crafted fables of all: "Things would be perfect if. . .". You might end that phrase, "if I were a size 4" or "size 6," or perhaps for you, "size 16" would be perfection. This promise of a happy, easy, carefree life after losing weight is carefully hidden under many "fat-free" product labels, or between the covers of the latest diet book.

"Perfect" is exactly what some of us are aiming for:

I will never be 100% comfortable with my body until it is 100% perfect, and of course it never will be. I wish I could overcome this . . .

Lisa from Connecticut

Many of us identify with this desire for perfection. Notice her use of "100%" — no room for error there! We don't just want to be comfortable, we want to be 100% comfortable. We don't want to be merely perfect, but guaranteed-absolutely-positively perfect. With such a high standard, we can be certain that comfort and perfection will permanently elude us.

Please reinforce this message: quit trying to be perfect in every area and love yourself just the way you are. Also, quit judging others who aren't perfect either.

Barbara from Ohio

Gotcha, Barbara. That's exactly the direction we're moving toward.

What Every Woman Wants

A promotional letter from an organization called The Winning Woman advertised a cassette on raising your self-esteem with this opening statement:

She was over twenty, overweight and overwhelmed by feelings of insecurity and inferiority. She knew she'd failed at work, at marriage, at family relationships, at everything.

My friend Anne, who sent me a copy of this "winning" offer, jotted down two valid questions in the margin:

1. If this were a man, would they have been as likely to point out that he was "overweight?"
2. Is this meant to infer that if a woman is overweight, she is a failure at work, marriage, family . . . at everything?

These subtle (and not so subtle!) messages bombard us every day, in magazines, on television, even in our mailboxes. The life style improvements ascribed to bodily perfection are endless: greater happiness, professional success, attention from the opposite sex, ease in shopping, more money in the bank, even cuter kids.

The definition of the perfect body keeps moving down the scale, and not in our direction. In the early 60's, the average model weighed just 8% less than the average American woman. In the late 80's, the average model weighed 23% below the average weight of American women.[2]

Not a good trend.

Miss Perfect on Campus

The desire for a model-thin body has kept many women from pursuing their dreams.

> *When I was in high school, our state's largest newspaper used to print photographs of pretty, slender co-eds at our state's colleges every week. I was so convinced I wouldn't fit in there because I was fat that I never tried to get a college education.*
>
> Pat from Wisconsin

This is a heartbreaking comment to read, because the situation was so avoidable. If only someone had been an advocate for this woman in her post high school years. If only a sister, friend or parent had stepped in and said, "You can do this!" It might have made all the difference for Pat and many others of us.

My own college degree was handed to me in May 1990, a full fourteen years after most of my high school buddies graduated from college. I'd simply been too busy with my radio career and didn't bother to finish my college education. When I finally went back to college in 1986, I found it to be altogether fun, fairly challenging, and highly worthwhile.

True confession: I did not fit in those wrap-around classroom desks, especially when I was pregnant in 1987 and 1989! No problem. I just brought in a regular straight back chair from another room. You can adapt. If you aren't embarrassed about making such concessions, no one else will even notice or care.

When I graduated on Mother's Day 1990, I wore the flat hat with the tassel and the black graduation robe. It was, of course, "One Size Fits All!" Actually, I'm probably the only graduate whose gown really was my size. It zipped right up and fit like a dream. (I would have worn it home, but solid black is not my color!)

Did it feel good to earn that bachelor of arts in English after eighteen years and three colleges? You bet. Did I have a perfect 4. 0 grade point average? Heavens no! I did my best, earned perfectly fine (though not perfect) grades, and most important of all, graduated. As in many things in life, the key is to get it done, to the best of your ability. Period.

Not-So-Perfect Is Still Terrific

One woman's stumbling block — being less than perfect — is another woman's key to success:

> *My imperfection makes me more accessible and safe to admit "fears" to. I am less threatening.*
>
> Sandra from Missouri

My own experience as a speaker bears that out. Complete strangers come up and throw their arms around me after one of my presentations. What fun to give them such "permission!" I suppose it is a combination of body language, demeanor, dress, or style. But they can see I'm not perfect, don't expect *them* to be perfect, and that I'm there to help them have a good time. (Plus, I have a very huggable body, just like you do!)

Some of us have at least one perfect attribute:

> *Everyone makes fun of me because I'm a perfect hair person. It's like they never see the rest of me. My favorite comment is that if I took as much time worrying about my rear end as I do my hair, I'd have the best looking rear end in town!*
>
> Gail from Kentucky

Now, there's a woman I can relate to: funny and human. That's something we can all aspire to!

A Sizeable Impact at Work

It's one thing to want to be perfect for yourself. I don't advocate it, but at least it's your choice. What is definitely a no-no is when an employer expects you to meet some standard of perfection concerning appearance that has nothing whatsoever to do with your job performance.

One of the most revealing questions on my survey for this book was, "Does your size have any impact on your job? If so, please explain." Here are their responses. (Prepare to get angry!)

> *I believe that I was passed over for a job for someone with the same qualifications, but less experience, because of my "image."*
> Kitty from Kentucky

Many employers hide behind the word "image" because it is conveniently vague. While I am all in favor of dressing well and looking our best, our body size and shape and facial characteristics should never enter into the job placement picture.

But, they *do* enter into the picture, in subtle and not so subtle ways. Dr. Esther Rothblum conducted an employment study at the University of Vermont. Students were given identical job resumes, one with the photo of a woman weighing about 120 pounds, the other with a photo of a woman who weighed 150 pounds. Hardly a large woman, just a bit heavier than the social norm. The students' response? They consistently rated the 150-pound woman as lower on supervisory potential, self-discipline, professional appearance, personal hygiene, and determined that she deserved a lower starting salary![3] All this because of thirty pounds? Two dress sizes? Unfortunately, yes.

In the workplace we are, without a doubt, up against deeply ingrained misconceptions and old stereotypes that won't go away. We've seen such struggles before:

> *Back around 1945 when discrimination was raging, I had two strikes against me: I was black and I was fat. I was only seventeen-years-old. The pressure made me suicidal.*
> Martha from Ohio

That reminds me of a statement former Congresswoman Shirley Chisholm once made. She said that between being black and being female, being female was the greater challenge to her career. For Martha, being large may have been a third, even greater challenge. My hat is off to her for not only surviving, but thriving!

The competition in the workplace today is volatile enough without tossing in the size issue. But let's face it, size is an issue.

I think I have to work harder to win people over by being either knowledgeable, very nice and sincere, or funny.

Joyce from Virginia

Job discrimination because of size is a serious problem, one that was being addressed at various national levels even as I was writing this book. In the meantime, I firmly believe that our best defense is a positive offense. A woman who is confident about her knowledge and skills will project that confidence far beyond the boundaries of her body.

A Dilemma in Women's Health

Much of the work I do as a professional speaker is in the field of health care. Nurses, technicians, medically related associations, and hospital-sponsored events for the public are some of the health-oriented audiences I have the privilege of addressing each year.

Many of my clients kindly completed surveys for this book, and I was surprised to see a very definite pattern to their answers concerning, "Does your size affect your job?" These are all women, employed specifically in women's health departments, usually as R.N.'s or directors. Here are some of their replies, with names omitted (since they *are* my clients!). Note the similarities in their answers, which I've taken the liberty of capitalizing:

The PERCEPTION is that people in the health care field should be thin, trim and the PICTURE of health.

People PERCEIVE or think because I'm in health education I should be perfect. Perfect body, perfect eating and exercise habits, non-smoker.

I didn't get a job as a nurse recruiter because they felt my IMAGE wasn't what they wanted projected from the hospital.

It's essential to LOOK fit and healthy when you work in health care.

APPEARANCE is very important. (Especially when representing a hospital.)

If I FEEL overweight, I think I am delivering an unhealthy message to my clients. (This is the result of brainwashing, I know.)

Oh, dear friend, you are quite correct there! If these women had stated, "I must have low blood pressure, a healthy heart and low cholesterol levels to do this job," we might think it unusual. But we could at least say, "well, they must be in good health to help others be healthy." That's not reality, but it would at least make sense. Yet, none of them said they had to *be* healthy, just *look* healthy (read: thin).

Am I blaming these fine professionals? Not in the least. They are the product of the same society we are, one that equates perfectly thin bodies with perfect health, imperfect-looking bodies with imperfect health. One thin counselor who works with women struggles with what almost amounts to reverse discrimination because of her "image":

> *My big, beautiful clients hate me; and my narrow, nervous, eating-disordered (anorexic) clients think I'm just like them. Clients often assume that I'm "perfect" because they think my size is "perfect."*
>
> Cindy from Missouri

Or, how would you like to be a lecturer for a weight loss center and live up to these requirements?

> *I must remain within 4 pounds of goal weight or risk losing my job. It's hard to focus on whether you even feel well when you have a constant pink slip in your future.*
>
> Cynthia from Michigan

We have a long way to go, in health care and every other profession, toward ending size discrimination. After all, our goal is for everyone to *be* healthy, not just look the part.

Our Own Worst Enemies

Without question, there are whole professions that are size-biased, and some individual employers as well. There are times, however, when we "shoot ourselves in the foot," as my husband likes to say. By believing so completely that only thin women can compete in the workplace, we stop believing in ourselves.

*I may hesitate to approach a potential client because of insecure
feelings about the reaction to me.*

                                                      Louise from Georgia

It's easy to brush away such concerns on paper. But, we all know
Louise's hesitance is common. The trick is to develop sufficient body
confidence to handle such insecurities head-on.

You'll hear it again and again in these pages: People will accept
you only to the extent you accept yourself. If you have confidence in
your abilities, they may have confidence in you too. I've spent ten
years moving from holding back to pushing full steam ahead, and I'm
here to tell you: it's up to you!

Practical Considerations

Even if you have all the confidence a woman could want, there
are still some everyday hassles that need to be addressed when you're
venturing forth into a world made for smaller people.

I think the audience may not accept or believe me if I'm too big.

                                                      Patty from California

This wonderful woman also happens to be a professional speaker
(and a friend). The part about the "audience may not accept or believe
me" fascinated me because that's not been my own experience at all.
I think attitude is everything. I accept myself and dress appropriately.
Audiences always applaud enthusiastically, and sometimes they stand
up! I take that as acceptance of both the message and the messenger.

Then again, another speaker who conducts training sessions got
this reaction from someone in her audience:

*One day my husband came home from work and was telling me
what one of his colleagues said about me. His coworker mentioned
how smart I was and that as soon as I started talking, people started
listening and didn't even think about what I looked like.*

                                                      Joyce from Virginia

Her husband thought it was meant to be a compliment, and it was.
Sort of.

Here are some other practical concerns women voiced about life on the job:

Getting around hospital furniture and physical therapy equipment is hard.

Andi from California

And, many of us can identify with this woman's challenge.

Getting in and out of my car is difficult in a compact car space in the parking structure.

Mary Ann from California

These things are definitely a nuisance. In some cases, we can simply arrange things to make life easier for ourselves and other larger people. Or, we may just need to enlist someone else for assistance:

Every time something is needed that's in a "tight" spot — I'm elected to "squeeze" in and get it because I'm a size 6!

Mary Anne from Indiana

I am always grateful when I'm seated next to the Mary Anne's of the world when I'm in this situation:

I'm embarrassed on airplanes because my arms touch the other person.

Janice from Idaho

Oh, Janice! I could do a twenty-minute routine on my experiences with airline seats. As a frequent flyer on six carriers, let me offer some words of wisdom for handling the hassle of flying.

Helping Delta Be "Ready When You Are"

Here are a dozen tips for making air travel more bearable, even enjoyable:

1. Use a great travel agent, someone who knows the business and is empathetic to your needs. If you aren't already a frequent flyer on the airline with the most flights in and out of your nearest airport, fill out their simple form

now. It doesn't cost a dime, and I've found that being a Delta Royal Medallion Member gets me extra good service.

2. Book thirty days in advance for the best choice of seats (and usually, the lowest airfares).

3. Get an aisle seat on the three-seat side, as close to the front as possible, but *not* the bulkhead seat. (They have solid stationary sides.) Ask for a row that doesn't have a passenger seated in the middle seat. (They can't guarantee it will remain that way, but you can at least begin with the best situation.)

4. Try to fly during off times (middle of the week, middle of the day, Saturdays) rather than the busiest times (mornings, Fridays). There is always more room and better service when you're not flying peak.

5. Arrive at the gate at least thirty minutes before the scheduled departure time. When the agent is checking your ticket, ask, "Is the seat in the middle still vacant?" I usually have a little fun with them, and add, "You see, I like to travel with both my hips, and thought I'd see if there's room for them today!" They always laugh, and they always help me if they can. They'll usually move me to an empty row. On four occasions they've moved me up to First Class at no extra charge, just to be nice! (Don't hold your breath for this. That's four times out of hundreds of flights.) The only time they can't move me is when the flight is booked solid.

6. When you find your seat, get everything up in the overhead compartment so you have as much room around you as possible.

7. Push up the arm rest. If someone is seated in that middle seat (ugh), I say something like, "We will probably both be a little more comfortable with this up. Would you mind?" Sometimes they do mind, most times they don't. It's worth asking.

8. Try the seat belt as soon as you sit down. If it won't extend enough for you, ask the flight attendant, before she gets busy, for a seat belt extension. It's actually one of those little demonstration belts and should help you breathe easier. For some reason, the seat belts on jets are bigger

than those on commuters. I just ask for one as I'm boarding the smaller planes, and they hand me one on the spot. I've never had them even look at me funny, let alone act rude or insensitive. These truly are professionals, and safety is their first concern.

9. When the middle seat is vacant, use that tray table for your soda and peanuts or the "snack" (i.e., frozen solid roll, limp roast beef, cheese wedge, tiny cracker, mushy apple. M-m-m...).

10. If all three seats in your row are vacant (you lucky soul!), then switch to the middle seat, and put up both arm rests. The center cushions are invariably softer (less use), and then the attendants won't accidentally crash their beverage cart into your elbow or knee. I flip all three tray tables down and have a branch office in the sky!

11. For hauling luggage, I use one of those little carts on wheels like the flight attendants use. If you fly even twice a year, you'll appreciate having one of these handy helpers. A good one will cost $35-$45, but will last for years.

12. Dress comfortably! I wear flats with cushioned soles, only a light coat year-round, and slacks or a split-skirt for more graceful bending over. Since I'm often met by a client, I send them a little poem that tells them what to expect when they meet me. It says:

> At the airport, should we meet,
> Here's the woman you will greet...
> I'll be tall, about five-nine,
> Yellow hair that's short and fine,
> Full of figure, eyes of blue,
> Fair of skin and glasses, too.
> Wearing flats and comfy clothes
> Don't forget those pantyhose!
> Luggage will be one black bag,
> On a rolling cart to drag.
> Smiling, laughing, waving, too —
> I'll be happy to see you!

It features a little caricature of me, so the person meeting me will know me on sight. It also lists the arrival date, time and flight. Just a simple thing, but it takes away some of those meeting-somebody-for-the-first-time jitters.

Go to the Head of the Class

Even if your job doesn't require air travel, your size may mean some similar challenge must be met:

> *It makes it more difficult to haul in my supplies for teaching. I always hope they'll put my class on a ground floor, next to the outside door, by a close parking lot!*
>
> Pat from Wisconsin

Maybe that luggage cart would help here. My guess is, *thin* teachers hope for the same thing. I love this woman's experience:

> *I work with two other teachers — same age as me, but sizes 6 and 8. One day at the end of our classes a sweet little eight-year-old girl gave each of us a hug. She looked at me quite politely and said, "Mmmm! You're soft!"*
>
> Barbara from Pennsylvania

One teacher said that her size did indeed impact her job, because her very presence could "scare the most troublesome kids to death!" Here is another woman who makes the most of her abundant talents:

> *I think my size is reassuring and non-threatening. Occasionally I will have an individual who initially is distant, but I have this wonderful smile and a southern accent. I use them both!*
>
> LaDonna from Oregon

A Skinny Voice

I'm already a fan of a woman named Cookie. She's a sales representative who spends a lot of time on the phone. Size is not an issue for her on the job:

> *I don't have any problem because I have a skinny, young voice!*
>
> Cookie from Texas

Funny you should say that, Cookie. That's what I heard from people back when I was a radio personality. My career on the air spanned ten years (1978-88), seven stations with all kinds of formats (jazz, top 40, disco, album rock, country, oldies, and adult contemporary), in five states (Pennsylvania, Maryland, Indiana, Michigan and Kentucky).

The one constant in all that craziness was that people thought I sounded thin. (What exactly does a thin person sound like?) My voice is fairly low for a woman, and somewhat musical. In fact, one time I had a listener complain about "that woman on the air who sounds like a piano!" Most people were much kinder and said my voice was mellifluous. This I know: many clients were delighted to have me voice their commercials and could have cared less what size or shape I was.

But my regular listeners cared very much. They wanted me to fit an imaginary picture of Liz they had in their mind's eye. When they would finally meet me in person at a promotional event, their responses were pretty predictable:

"Gee whiz! You don't look like you sound!"

"I thought you'd be thinner!"

"Are you sure you're Lizzie?" (No. I'm Cher.)

And, my personal favorite:

"You don't sound *fat* on the radio!"

That one left me speechless (which doesn't happen very often!). Later, I thought of a brilliant comeback: "Ma'am, the Bible says that my body is a temple of the Holy Spirit. He just started a building program that got out of hand!"
(Why can't we come up with that stuff when we need it?)

My Radio Studio "Closet"

To be honest, radio was a great place to hide. I could be a sultry siren or a sophisticated career woman or a young ingenue, and no one was the wiser. With only my voice to work with, I could be anything I wanted. I tried all of the above, with limited success.

My real success in radio came when I was just myself on the air, telling stories and sharing my struggles and discoveries. Still, I was only a voice without a body, an invisible woman.

> *I feel that many women become overweight to become invisible. Society tends to look past and ignore large women. It's safe. A place no one will hurt you anymore, because they don't pay attention to you.*
>
> Sandra from Missouri

I think radio was, initially, safe for me. My last station, one of the finest 50,000-watt clear channel outlets in the country, WHAS-AM in Louisville, was less safe. On-air personalities were expected to do lots of meeting and greeting and frequent promotional appearances. I had to play the music, and face the music when I stepped out of the studio each day.

As scary as that was, it was also the very thing that led me into professional speaking. From 1983 on, people began inviting me to speak to their Kiwanis Club, their church group, their school assembly. Soon the number of calls had grown to ninety a year. Before long, it was obvious that I should move to platform speaking. Who could have guessed that what had once scared me most of all — public appearances — would soon become my main source of income and my favorite way to spend the day?

No More Hiding

I began my speaking business in 1987, with one foot still in radio (in case I "bombed!"). My business grew slowly at first. Not every engagement was fun. I remember standing behind a group of folks at a banquet, trying to think of what I might say to invite myself into their circle. I heard one of the men in the group say, "Hey, have you seen Liz yet? She's a big woman. I mean a B-I-G woman!" Everyone laughed and started looking around. As you might imagine, I wanted to crawl out of that room and never speak publicly again!

But I lived through that night, and many since then. Because my promotional brochure and photos clearly show my clients that I'm a "large and lovely" speaker, they're never surprised. And, since they usually use my photos in their promotion of the event, the audience is seldom taken aback either.

To act as an icebreaker, and to address the size issue immediately, I have some fun with my size as soon as I pick up the microphone. Then we're on to other things. I have found audiences don't want a "perfect" speaker — how intimidating! — but they do want a speaker who is perfectly happy with who she is. Finally, I can say I am.

The conventional wisdom in the speaking profession is "the audience will feel what you feel." I focus on feeling joyful, confident and relaxed. Then, I watch people take on those same attributes. I believe you can apply that same simple formula where you work.

Lest you think I've got it all together on this confidence thing, I'll let you in on some instances when my confidence slipped just a tad.

Sizing Up to the Truth

I delayed designing my first fancy brochure for several months, because I kept thinking (you won't believe this), "Maybe I could lose a few pounds before I visit the photographer." Talk about denial!

An agent I was working with just shook his head when I tried to explain this delay. "Listen to your own message, Liz!" he rightfully told me. The photos were taken. Soon my very own red, black, and ivory brochures came rolling off the press. Ta-da!

I mailed copies of my new brochure to some friends in the business and waited for their glowing remarks. They came. But so did a letter from a special friend, Rosita Perez. She wrote: "In your new brochure, you call yourself a 'Size 16 Tinkerbell.' Liz, having cut the labels out of a few 18's myself, I just cannot believe that you are anything less than an 18 or 20." There was no point to being either mad or offended. First of all, I trust her completely, and second of all, she was right. Well, I did have one size 16 dress that still fit — after a fashion. It had an elastic waist. But most of my clothes were indeed 18's and 20's.

Her letter continued. "I care too much about your success, Liz. The problem is, if the audience does not believe you, it may ruin your credibility in all else that you share." That was the real problem here. Not the dress size, forget that. It was my reputation, my trustworthiness that was important. Rosita knew it, and she loved me enough to confront me. Say what you will, that's a real friend.

I have a new brochure now (with no dress size listed at all), and from the platform I call myself, accurately, a size 22 Tinkerbell. (Just for the record, there are a few 24's in the closet too!) Thanks, Rosita, for making an honest woman out of me.

What I've learned after five hundred professional presentations over the last several years is that success is built on credibility, confrontation and communication. In any endeavor, if we're willing to be true to ourselves, confront untruth when we see it, and share the truth as we know it, amazing things will happen.

A Strategy for Success

I had another "a-ha!" experience in 1990 when I enlisted the services of a strategic planning expert to help me map out my speaking business for the next five years. Stephen Tweed asked me a simple question: "What is your competitive advantage? What makes you unique?"

Without hesitation, I blurted out, "I'm a big, beautiful woman!" Soon I thought of other things: I'm funny and love helping women laugh, I enjoy the selling process, serving my clients, and so on. But the first advantage that came to mind was my size.

Imagine that. What I once considered my biggest problem I now considered to be one of my biggest pluses!

Here are three reasons why I believe any large woman can use her size to her advantage in business (I call this my 3-M theory):

1. Few people have ever seen a big woman standing proud, smiling at the world, employing her gifts, and living life to the fullest without apology. You will, therefore, be MIRACULOUS to people!
2. Because of your uniqueness, you will be MEMORABLE. My clients and audiences may remember me as "that big, funny blonde woman," but they do remember me. They will remember you too!
3. As any marketing expert will tell you, an unusual and identifiable product is very MARKETABLE ... that's you! Any products or services that you provide will sell themselves, because you are sold on you, and so are your buyers.

I used to worry that I alone subscribed to my 3-M theory, and therefore it must be faulty. But each year I meet more women who've learned the same lessons and come to the same conclusion:

[Some folks] think that big people — women in particular — are not in control. The joke's on them. Sometimes our very size puts us in control!

Anne from South Carolina

The Perfect Role Model

It's exciting to find people who are further down the road on this particular journey. Such role models can show us where the potholes are, the smoother paths, the hidden stumbling blocks. We need each other!

I live in a very small town and I need to hear about overweight women who have become successful in their careers and lives, who have been pioneers, so to speak, and done things other people may not have done, even people of normal weight.

Pat from Wisconsin

Let me tell you about Linda, an amazing woman I met while doing a presentation in eastern Pennsylvania. After the program was over, I shook hands and gave hugs and greeted the wonderful members of my audience.

That's when I saw Linda, aboard her mobility aid, waiting on the sidelines to talk to me. She is a big, beautiful woman, with the emphasis on beautiful. Linda has conquered cancer, owns her own business, and volunteers as a fireman and emergency medical responder. Incredible! As she puts it:

Someone whose house is on fire, or who has been in an accident and is bleeding, does not care whether I'm fat, skinny, ugly or beautiful. They just need help!

You might wonder, as I did, how a large woman who isn't able to walk because of various physical challenges, might be of service in an emergency. Here's how:

When the alarm sounds, the adrenal rush blocks all pain, at least for awhile. At fire scenes, I can make sure all the men are properly geared, change air bottles, hold a hose. Accident scenes are a little different. Out here in the boonies, I might have to wait an hour for more highly trained personnel to arrive. Sometimes I go home and straight to bed with my Advil, heating pad, hot water bottle and ice

*pack. The pain eventually goes away. There is such a tremendous
satisfaction in knowing I really counted for something, helped
someone in trouble and maybe even helped save a life! Nothing
compares with that!*

Talk about a positive attitude. Linda's heroic efforts would put
most of us to shame. Thankful to be alive, she sums it all up: "What's
a little fat among friends?" Perfect.

Begin Building Body Confidence Today

1. Begin replacing any "perfect" goals in your life with healthy,
   realistic goals. When possible, don't aim for a number.
   Make your goals small, manageable, measurable (but not
   in pounds and inches).

2. If there is something you've been putting off until you could
   do it "perfectly" or until the "perfect time," ask yourself,
   "Why not today?" Take one small step in that direction.

3. Make a list of three benefits of being your current size.

❤ *A Psychologist Speaks . . .*

Dr. Kathryn D. Cramer is director of The Cramer Institute in St. Louis, Missouri. She has both a master's degree and Ph.D. in psychology, with specialties in health psychology, adult development and organizational consulting. She is the author of *Staying on Top When Your World Turns Upside Down*, and *Forty, Get Set, Grow!*

Liz: What is the connection between the body image obsession many of us have and perfectionism?

Kathy: *No matter what our body type, many women experience a drive to be perfect through having a body that others find attractive. Our striving to be perfect has two dimensions — a self dimension and a social dimension. Our bodies are one of the most prominent means of interacting with one another. It's normal that someone whose internal standards are to strive for perfection would manifest that in terms of her attitude toward her body. And, it's not surprising that she would seek the approval of others to validate her achievement of that internal standard.*

Liz: Why do we set such high standards for ourselves?

Kathy: *The drive to be perfect is really a misguided but well-intentioned motive. Most of us develop our striving to be perfect out of our desire to please our parents and other authorities whom we depend on and love. It's very rare that we emerge from the womb with a desire to be perfect! When the authorities in our lives keep "raising the bar" in order for us to win their approval, the foundation of perfectionism is established.*

Liz: What leads women to believe that if they were just thinner — shorter, taller, prettier, younger, or older — they would be happier and/or more successful?

Kathy: *This is a frequent error most often made during the first half of life, or until a person reaches their mid-40's. Our culture promises that happiness can be achieved by amassing external, visible success. In America that means money, career, marital status, and the "light look." Most people go through some sort of mid-life awakening which conveys just how hollow this search for happiness along such external lines can be.*

Liz: Mid-life awakening sure beats having a mid-life crisis! What does it produce?

Kathy: *Those women who are open to the kind of wisdom which is truly possible only during the second half of life have a chance to correct such misconceptions. Genuine happiness is linked to the fulfillment of one's unique inner talents and potential and has little if anything to do with culturally defined success. However, up until now there have been very few guidelines for how to live a genuinely happy life.*

Liz: How can a woman change how she feels about herself, and be genuinely happy?

Kathy: *One of the most profoundly powerful tools in self-change is self-nurturing. If women will only apply to themselves the type of coaching and caring they give to their children and other people in need, they would begin to view themselves compassionately. This compassionate self-perception is the fundamental basis for self-change.*

Liz: In order for change to occur, how important is it for us to determine *why* we think, act and feel the way we do?

Kathy: *For some people, insight into their own motives and "blind spots" gives them a chance to make order out of chaos. Self-understanding should not be the only goal, but for many it is the key to being compassionate about themselves. Such insights are achieved layer by layer, like peeling an onion. Slowly, one begins to understand the complexities involved, especially with something as complex as bodily appearance. For many women, gaining insight into themselves is a powerful, positive step in taking charge of their lives.*

"Large Women Adore Wearing Double Knit" (It's So Flattering!)

There was a time when women's clothing left a lot to the imagination. Covering themselves with yards of fabric from neck to toe, women of another era used undergarments to give them the shape they wanted. Rather than dieting and exercise, stays and corsets were used to produce a tiny waist or slimmer torso. Of course, fashion designers of the last century also *added* to the female form with bustles and hoops. (Almost makes you want those antebellum fashions to come back for another round!)

Back then, big, beautiful women like Lillian Russell were revered. Known as America's sweetheart, she weighed in at 200 pounds by the early 1900's.[1] It wasn't long, however, until designers introduced a new style of dress that required a much leaner body. By 1908, *Vogue* was singing the praises of these new straight-skirted, high-waisted empire fashions: "How slim, how graceful, how elegant women look."[2] Full-figured women would never really be "in vogue" again.

With the new fashions came the necessity to reshape the female form, and so women started counting calories and weighing themselves at home. For the first time, we became number-obsessed. Two books published in 1917, both written by women, paved the way for diet books to follow: *Lose Weight and Be Well* and *Diet and Health, with Key to the Calories.*[3] It's interesting to me that, though new fashions were the impetus for this growing concern with being thin, health was touted as the reason to pursue slenderness. (The more things change, the more they stay the same.)

My mother, born in 1911, always said that the worst day of her life arrived with the advent of sack dresses in the 20's. Those straight, shapeless, just-below-the-knee dresses were not flattering to her full-figured body. They've come back in style from time to time, but never for long. They only look good on hangers and fashion models, not on most mothers.

"What Shall I Wear?"

Miss Manners said, "What shall I wear?" is society's second most frequently asked question. The first is "Do you really love me?"

Both questions are self-esteem issues. I believe if a woman truly loves herself and the body she lives in, she will choose what she wears with care, knowing that her outward attire is often a reflection of her inner being.

The balance between inner beauty and the more visible kind is precarious.

> Do not let your adornment be merely outward — arranging the hair, wearing gold, or putting on fine apparel — rather let it be the hidden person of the heart, with the incorruptible beauty of a gentle and quiet spirit, which is very precious in the sight of God.[4]

No question about it. A woman who is only beautiful on the outside is truly unattractive. If we think a hot new haircut, 24k gold jewelry or an expensive outfit is all it takes to be a beautiful woman, we're sadly mistaken. Haircuts grow out, jewelry is lost or stolen, clothing gets damaged or goes quickly out of style. That stuff *is* corruptible. It doesn't last.

But for a woman radiant on the inside to be dull as dishwater on the outside is also a sad waste of beauty. I have met more women who had gentle quiet spirits, drab clothing and sad faces than I can count.

All women, but especially larger women, need to get their inside and outside selves more in sync. Which one needs the most attention right now? If your outside self is gorgeous but your inner being has been neglected, start nurturing your spiritual self. If your spiritual self is beautifully gentle, then frame that with clothes that mirror your sweet spirit and radiate your light from within.

No "Omar the Tentmaker" Jokes, Please

It has taken years, even decades, but the garment industry has finally created decent fashions for larger women. What in the world took them so long? We've been waiting, credit cards clutched in our fists, for ages.

They've had retail stores for larger men since mid-century. These shops are very sensibly called "Big and Tall Men." The fellas just walk in, find what they need, plunk down their money and head out the door. No stigma attached, no clerk "tsk-tsking" outside the dressing room, no premium price for the larger sizes. Oh, maybe a few dollars extra for more fabric, but nothing outrageous.

Why didn't they create stores like that for women with fuller figures? Easy. They knew we would never walk in a store called "Big Fat Girls!"

So, they stayed up late at night in Merchant Land and came up with lots of euphemistic names for such stores: Added Dimensions. Pretty and Plump. Extra Special. Lots to Love. Large and Luscious. Twice as Nice. (I guess they have a line of Petites called "Half as Nice!") One of my favorites is Great Personality. You can just imagine a man saying, "Well, she may not be a size 10, but she has a great personality!"

Some of the names are quite lovely. Grande Lady has a nice ring to it. I found a Renoir's Lady in Portland that had terrific clothes at discounted prices. And I don't mind thinking of myself as a Rubenesque Woman. One of my favorite names is The Forgotten Woman. Oprah has shopped there. So has Roseanne. So has Lizzie, when I'm speaking in one of the nineteen cities that has The Forgotten Woman (and when I have some room left in my budget!).

Just for Us

*The "Women's" sizes are always tucked away out of sight . . . in
the back of the building next to customer service and the restrooms.
It's almost like they're ashamed of it.*

Joyce from Virginia

We've come a long way since those days (although in small towns
across the land, that's still the only option). The nicer stores for
women who wear sizes 14-26 carry everything we might ever need
(well, almost everything: "Where are boots for large women?" Judith
from Colorado rightly wants to know). They do carry swimsuits,
lingerie, business suits, casual clothes, even sequin-bedecked evening
gowns! Catherine from Kentucky said sequined dresses were out for
her because "I'm not made for slinky!"

Au contraire, my dear Catherine. At a wonderful store in
Oklahoma City, with your very name, "Catherine's," I found not one
but two gorgeous knee-length sequined dresses, one purple with gold,
one black with gold, very classy, my size and on sale.

You'll remember for years they called themselves Catherine's
Stout Shop. No more. They've scaled up their image, dropped the
Stout Shop part (though on some store marquees you can still faintly
see where the letters were). They've also designed a zingy new logo
and added the phrase, "Fashion independence for today's large size
woman." Hooray for Catherine's!

Two of the women who completed surveys for this book work in
stores for larger women. We made a deal: I bought some clothes, they
filled out a survey! Vicki lets us in on why such stores are the perfect
place to work:

*I need to be full-figured to work where I do! You can't put a size 8
clerk in our store and think a size 22 patron will seriously take a
compliment from them.*

Vicki from Wisconsin

That reminds me of a big, beautiful woman named Leslie who I
met at a convention. It seems the national president of her association
was coming to town and had asked Leslie to arrange a shopping trip
for her. Apparently the only chance this V.P. ever had to buy clothes
was when she traveled. She wanted this plus-size beauty to visit a few

stores in advance and have some suits ready for her to try on. The V.P. wore a size 2 or 4 petite.

"Liz," Leslie confided, her eyes twinkling, "can you imagine what these shop owners must have thought when I breezed in, grabbed half a dozen suits in sizes 2 and 4 petite, tossed them on the counter and said, 'Could you hold these for me? We'll be back to try them on at 3:00 P.M.'!"

Sometimes it's easier to catalogue shop: *Just My Size* for comfy sweats and pantyhose, *Silhouettes* for nice, affordable dresses, *Just Right!* for better dresses and suits, *Brownstone Woman* for classy career dressing and the *I. Magnin* catalogue when I just want to drool. You'll find more information about these and other catalogues in the resources section of this book.

Wherever you shop, be daring. Try something new, something that doesn't look like "you." More than once I have been surprised and delighted to find that some off-the-wall-looking outfit does fun things to my big body. You just never know. And, don't be afraid to put on a belt if the outfit calls for it. Carole Shaw of *BBW* magazine was one of the first people to suggest putting belts on larger fashions. Women protested, of course, saying, "But, we have no waist!" Carole makes it sound so simple: "Just bend over. Wherever you crack, that's your waist!"

I am short-waisted and long-legged, so I often have trouble finding pants that look, fit and feel right on my body. Recently I found one manufacturer who must have a mannequin built like me, because their pants fit me perfectly. Of course I bought three pairs: black, royal blue and (look out, world) orange! It's true: colors that compliment your skin and hair will make you look more polished, energetic, and comfortable with your twice-as-nice self.

Store-Bought Confidence

To a certain extent, one can "purchase" a healthy dose of body confidence. I love beautiful clothing, not only for how it makes me look, but how it makes me feel.

I choose things that feel good against my skin. Silk is my favorite, because of how it hangs and drapes, the way it floats and dances around me. As a natural fabric, it breathes, keeping me cool in the summer and warm in the winter. Wool makes me itch, but 100% cotton feels fabulous. Yes, you have to iron it, but after enough washings, it gets less wrinkled.

Clothes that feel good physically can help us feel good emotionally. I don't pretend to understand how this works psychologically, but I'm certain it is a universal experience.

Feeling good about the way I look makes me more confident in my ability.

Cynthia from New Jersey

When we feel that we look our best (*our* best, not someone else's definition) then we can face the world with a smile, confident we have something to offer.

Author Roberta Pollack Seid describes dressing as a "virtual process of self-creation, of self-portraiture. It reveals the way we see ourselves and the way we want others to see us."[5] Sometimes how others view us, though, doesn't accurately reflect the message we are trying hard to communicate:

People say to me, "You dress well for a woman of your size."

Kathryn from Arkansas

They were doing fine till they got to the "for a woman of your size" part. It's obvious they mean such things to be compliments, so the best thing to do is receive them as such. Vow to be more sensitive with others than some people are with you.

The truth is, a well-dressed 16+ woman stands out from the crowd, and I mean in the most positive sense. I tell people that I simply must dress well, in dramatic styles and bold colors, because I have such a large canvas to paint on. It would be a shame to waste one inch of it with something dull and drab!

There are many styles that you must be larger to pull off. I think the wedge dresses of recent years, and especially the swing jackets, look ridiculous with a pair of spider legs hanging out the bottom. You and I fill them out properly and give them panache.

Anne from South Carolina wonders, "Why do manufacturers think that big women want to wear faddish clothes, i.e., short hem lines and ruffles, regardless of how we look in them?"

A legitimate question, of course. Yet there are those of us who love how we look in the shorter skirts and ruffled hems. I'm just glad the fashion folks are giving us some choices, so we can decide. After all, ten women may all wear a size 20 dress and yet look very different in the same outfit. Height, build, and body proportions all factor into the fashion mix. The key is to find a few styles that always make you feel good, always get you sincere compliments. Then, seek out those special styles when you shop. I'm grateful for fashions that make us look well-dressed instead of like we're wearing a shower curtain!

Models and Mannequins

When larger women can look so smashing in the latest fashions, why do you suppose the garment industry insists on showing their clothes on very thin women? It's an aesthetic problem. Fashion designers don't want women's bodies to get in the way of their clothes. Instead, they want mannequins that move, dress racks that dance, hangers that have no "love handles" or anything else to distract the eye of the buyer.

You knew I'd have to mention Twiggy. She graced the cover of *Vogue* four times in 1967, the year I entered junior high and began my love/hate affair with dieting. She was 5'7". She weighed 91 pounds.[6] Even Twiggy herself said, "It's not what you would call a figure, is it?"[7]

No. Most mannequins haven't much of a figure either, averaging a 33 inch bust. The average American woman is at least 3 inches bigger, lots of us are 10 inches bigger. Sharlyne Powell, the founder of "Women At Large" and a producer of excellent exercise videos for larger women, was a guest on the Sally Jesse Rafael show recently. Sharlyne shared a telling statistic: Ten years ago, the average bra size for an American woman was a 34B. Now, it's a 36C. We are getting bigger, including in some of the "right" places.

Fashion Fables

A collection of fables has been passed down to us over the years, untruths which we now have to work through, so that dressing becomes fun again. For example, there's the classic, "Black is a slimming color." This is true if you're a penguin. For the rest of us, black turns our body into one giant, colorless shadow. This isn't to say black can't be made to look good on a larger woman. But it needs some shape, some contrast, some movement, or it will just sit there.

Here's another favorite fable: "Stripes make you look thinner." Can't you hear your mother intoning this one from outside your dressing room while you tried on that striped dress she chose? Vertically striped, of course.

As you might guess, the winning fable at our house is, "One size fits all!" All what? All one leg? Ione from Michigan suggests, "Why don't they make one size fits all tent dresses that can be cut off for any height?" (Isn't that a picture?)

"One size fits all" is such a fashion fable that whenever my book title is announced as part of my introduction before a speech, the audience laughs. Rightly so. It *is* laughable, although not in every situation:

> *One New Year's Eve in an emergency situation I was forced to purchase a pair of "Chubby Chick" pantyhose which were "One Size Fits All." Needless to say, pulling them on and [having them] reach only the top of the thigh made for a very uncomfortable evening.*
>
> Merkin from Pennsylvania

Here are some insights from a smaller sister, a woman for whom "one size fits all" is a fallacy too:

> *I'm 5'3", 93 pounds, with a 24 inch waist. I'm also thirty-six years old and the mother of four children, ages eight to fifteen. I have to find my clothes in the children's department, or buy a girl's size 12 pattern then fight to find fabric that doesn't make it look like a child's dress.*
>
> Danise from Ohio

So much for "life must be easier for petites!"

How Can an 18 and a 38 Be the Same Size?

When I asked women to tell me their dress size, some had trouble answering, and no wonder. Clothing manufacturers can't seem to decide if we are 18-20-22-24-26 or 38-40-42-44-46. For most of us, you can forget suits or any combinations that are sold together. Our bodies aren't made that way. We much prefer to buy such pieces separately.

One label in particular gave me a big giggle: I bought a two-piece suit with a split skirt, and was amazed to discover the label clearly said, Petite. It actually fit very well, because of my short waist. Even so, a size 24 Women's Petite seems a contradiction in terms. I must say, I delight in showing the label to my tiny friends, and saying "See? I'm a Petite too!"

Women have sent me dress labels that are equally amusing. One casual outfit sported a tag clearly labeled "2X-Medium." What fun to be a Medium again!

Sometimes, we don't want anyone to know what size we wear. One woman admitted, "I still cut my old underwear up into many pieces before I throw them away so no one can laugh if they happen to find them at the dump." I must admit, I cut the labels out of my own 100% cotton, full-size briefs the minute I take them out of the package, but only because the labels irritate my skin. Or maybe, like this honest woman, I'd rather not have anyone know I wear 4x underwear. (I mean, what would they say in the hospital emergency room?)

Another woman shared her struggles with shopping with a smaller daughter:

My teenage daughter likes for me to go shopping with her. I wait while she selects her size 7's and tries them on and models them. I watch smaller mothers with their daughters trying on the same outfits and sharing dressing rooms and I become depressed. I hate to shop.

Joyce from Virginia

There's no question about it, the word "dressed" is only two letters away from "depressed!" How about a shopping trip for mom to *her* kind of store with *her* clothes, while daughter watches, comments and applauds? It might be a good learning experience for her.

I always prefer to shop alone, with a great sales clerk to help me try things I might otherwise overlook. I've also shopped with my big, beautiful friend Ann, who talked me into purchasing my first outrageously colorful hand-painted silk dress. She was so right . . . I wear it all the time.

Cleaning Your Closets

Let's talk about your closet for a minute. Do you have whole racks filled with clothes, which haven't fit you in five or ten years or more? If you're ready to take a big step, I have an idea for you to consider: GET RID OF THOSE CLOTHES!

Why? They take up valuable closet space. They're going out of style and becoming less useful to someone (especially you) every season they hang there. They're a constant reminder that you're no longer wearing size 10 (or 6 or 14 or whatever). It's time to clean house. Here's how I did it:

1. I hung all the clothing by sizes in my basement on a big wheel-around rack (we picked it up for a song — $25 — when a local discount store went out of business). There they were, hundreds of dollars worth of stylish clothing in sizes 10, 12, 14, 16, 18. (Sigh.) Don't make the mistake that I did, of holding your old skirts up to your hips and getting bummed out. Life is too short. Out with the small, in with the new!

2. Taking a deep breath, I invited smaller friends, one by one, to come over and go "shopping." Yes, a consignment shop might have been less traumatic, but it is also made a clear statement to those who love me most: I am who I am, and I'm not likely to ever be a size 10 again. It's very freeing to make this kind of public "confession."

3. I rejoiced when I saw my friends sporting my old favorites. Believe it or not, this was a very healing thing for me. It's also a practical move, and good stewardship to boot. Now, those good clothes are being put to use, instead of making faces at me every time I open the closet door. My friends were thrilled, and it made lots more room in my closets.

If you're still hesitating, thinking "maybe someday these will fit me again," let's be realistic. If you were to, quite by accident, lose a lot of weight, do you really think you'd go back to wearing clothes, colors and fabrics from five or ten years ago? Heck no, you'd want to go out and buy a bunch of new clothes to celebrate your new (though probably temporary) body. Trust me: It's better to get rid of your old clothes, buy some beauties in the size that fits you today, and sally forth!

"Figure Flaws" My Foot!

I'll never forget the poolside fashion show I once attended, which was described in the program as "How to Find a Swimsuit to Flatter Every Figure." Sounded good to me, so I sat near the front and waited to see what I might learn. The first model came out. A size 6. The fashion commentator began: "As you can see, Carol's hips are much bigger than her shoulders, and this suit helps camouflage her out-of-proportion body."

A faint rumbling sound moved through the audience of 250 women. I felt sorry for poor Carol up there, having her hips discussed in such an impersonal, public way, especially when she had (compared to most of us in the audience) no visible hips whatsoever.

The second model came out. Another size 6. "Here is Joanie in a slimming black suit that accentuates her slim torso, but plays down her larger backside." Larger than what? Larger than a bread box, maybe, but smaller than any backside I'd seen in years!

It was soon apparent that all the models were going to be a size 6, that their "figure flaws" existed only in the mind of the commentator, and that the women in the audience were about to explode. Finally, they did. They exploded in laughter.

A word of warning for all fashion industry types: we never want to hear about "How to Hide Your Figure Flaws" again! Our figures are not flawed, they are uniquely ours, all different, and wonderful "as is." Stop asking us to change our bodies to fit your clothes, and start changing your clothes to fit our bodies!

Begin Building Body Confidence Today

1. Look through your current wardrobe and determine your favorite style of clothing — your best colors, fabrics and styles. Make a list, even a sketch, of what you like best, and keep it handy when you shop, along with a list of things you really need to complete an outfit. You'll shop smarter and faster!
2. Call a good dress store or sewing shop and locate a skilled, sensitive seamstress who can alter any clothes you have now to make them fit you better. She can also lower or shorten hems and cuffs on new outfits as soon as you bring them home, and she might be able to create some original, one-of-a-kind outfits for you based on your list of favorites.
3. Check the resources section of this book and have some of those catalogues delivered to your door. No salesman will call! Then, go ahead and try something totally "not you" and see if it isn't indeed the *new* you!

♥ *A Clothing Store Owner Speaks . . .*

Nancye Radmin is the founder and owner of The Forgotten Woman, a store with top-of-the-line fashions for larger women, located in nineteen cities across America. According to *Working Woman* magazine, The Forgotten Woman does $40 million a year in business.

Liz: Where did the name "The Forgotten Woman" come from?

Nancye: *Sixteen years ago, after giving birth to my son William, I had gained 85 pounds. So I went shopping. Understand, I am a clothes horse, only wore Anne Klein, that kind of thing. I went to my regular store, walked up to my favorite sales lady, and her first words were "What have you done to yourself?" I started bubbling about my new son, how thrilled we were, and she said, "I can't do anything for you until you lose weight." I never stepped in that store again.*

Liz: Many of us can identify with that experience! Then what happened?

Nancye: *I went across the street to another favorite store. Now, what I wanted was not that unusual. Navy gabardine pants, a cream blazer, and a yellow cashmere sweater. That's what everybody was wearing that year, so that's what I wanted. Of course, that store didn't have anything in my size either, and I was only a 14-16. They sent me to Elizabeth Arden, which had a wonderful collection of caftans. I wasn't interested. They sent me to B. Altman's, which featured house dresses. They sent me to Macy's, where I got a nose bleed getting up to the ninth floor to the larger women's sizes. They were right next to the pet center. Amid the squawking and the barking, I found a sea of polyester pull-on pants in four colors: navy, burgundy, black and brown. Stunning. In the same department they had coordinating polyester tops with big flowers. They looked exactly like the maternity clothes I had been wearing for the last nine months.*

Liz: Let me guess. You were fairly discouraged at this point.

Nancye: *Absolutely. I went home, having spent a total of $9.75, and that was just for parking. I had a pocketbook full of money and all the plastic I needed, but no clothes. I turned to my husband and said, "I am a forgotten woman! You have to give me $10,000. I am going to open a store that sells pretty clothes for fat girls." And that's how The Forgotten Woman was born. We opened our first store in May 1977, on Lexington Avenue in New York.*

Liz: You now have nineteen locations in all. Will you be adding more stores?

Nancye: *Probably in 1994. We'd love to bring The Forgotten Woman to Cincinnati.*

Liz: Hooray, that's near Louisville! You have your own "Nancye" label, yes?

Nancye: *That happened because no one in America was willing to manufacture gabardine clothing for me, so I headed to Brazil. The manufacturer asked me, "Where are your labels?" I had never thought of bringing such a thing with me, so I signed my name, and they made labels for me from my signature.*

Liz: Is there anything today's large woman can't buy for herself, clothing-wise?

Nancye: *Well, she can't buy Anne Klein or Donna Karan. Yet. These designers are not ready to create clothing for the larger woman. It seems their smaller customers are worried that they might be wearing something a larger woman is wearing. I don't understand what the problem is — we all wear the same shoes, carry the same handbags, drive the same cars! When designers have nowhere else to go, they finally think "fat."*

Liz: Why do large size fashions cost more?

Nancye: *Because you have to have a separate pattern made. You can't just "grade up" a smaller pattern or your shoulders would reach out to Asia and your crotch down to China! For example, a size 20 skirt requires about 20%*

more fabric than a size 8 skirt, and about 60% more stitches per inch. These things just cost more. In a bakery, a bigger cake always costs more than a smaller one.

Liz: What makes The Forgotten Woman distinctive?

Nancye: *I always insist on excellent service, and I only carry clothes that I would wear, the beautiful clothes smaller women are wearing. After all, we deserve the best. That's why we have never had a polyester pull-on pant out on the floor . . . and we never will!*

Liz: I also love your dress sizes: 1 through 6!

Nancye: *That's right. The size 14's are a 1, the 16's a 2, right up to 24 at a size 6. My customers tell me they love to drape their jackets over a chair, so that the label clearly shows they wear a size 4!*

"You'll Love Yourself More If You Lose Weight"

Self-image, as the phrase implies, refers to the image, concept or mental picture you have of yourself. It's not how you look, it's how you *think* you look. It's not who you really are, but rather, who you *think* you are.

In his book *His Image, My Image*, author Josh McDowell makes a telling point: "If you can think of anyone you'd rather be than yourself, you probably have a self-image problem."[1] Most of us have travelled that road, and it starts at a very young age.

All through grade school I wanted to be Donna — small, dark-haired, quiet. All through junior high I wanted to be Debbie — petite, cheerleader, the first in our gang to date. All through high school I wanted to be Judy — tall, thin, long brown hair, great big smile.

They were special young women and good friends, but for heaven's sake, what was wrong with Lizzie? I had my own gifts and skills to offer, my own happy smile and sense of humor to bring to the table. But I was not "cute," according to the politically correct version of "cute" in the 60's, and so I was miserable.

In the 90's, we are finding some solutions to such misery. Santa Cruz County, California, has a Task Force to Promote Self-Esteem and Personal and Social Responsibility. Their chairperson, Ardena Shankar, offered this definition of self-esteem: "Appreciation of my own worth and importance, and having the character to be accountable for myself and to act responsibly toward others."[2]

Sure sounds mighty Biblical to me! The Lord, without a doubt, "appreciates our worth and importance," calls us to be "accountable" and expects us to act "responsibly."

Notice how self-esteem, by this definition, has nothing to do with appearance, dress size, or level of "cute." Self-esteem based on such a flimsy foundation could be blown away with one tight button on your skirt. That's why the promise that "you'll love yourself more if you lose weight" is so dangerous. The corollary is, "and if you gain it back, you'll hate yourself forever."

When I became a Christian in 1982, I bought into the "looking good = feeling good = being good" philosophy that was being pandered about those days. I put my own little spiritual twist on it, just for grins. At that time, I was flirting with the 200-pound mark, with few attractive clothes to cover my growing self. So off I went to Weight Watchers again, only this time I told myself I would give God the glory for any changes that took place. Sure enough, my weight came off smoothly, easily and quickly. At 155, I was a svelte size 10 and a smash at church.

"Start a weight loss group!" everyone clamored, and so I did. I called it "WILL POWER," which stood for "My WILL Surrendered to God's POWER." There were lots of similar programs available in Christian circles in those days: 3-D, Overeaters Victorious, The Workshop in Lenten Living and others. Books on the topic filled the shelves of Christian bookstores: *Slim for Him, Free to Be Thin, Weight! A Better Way to Lose* and *More of Jesus, Less of Me.*

Before I tell you all the things that were wrong with WILL POWER, let me share a few "right" things. First of all, it brought me closer to God. Studying the Scriptures and writing messages for our weekly classes helped me get rooted and grounded in my faith as a new believer. I'm most grateful for that. It also got me standing up in front of small groups, which gave me the confidence I needed to begin my speaking career a few years later.

Third, it brought many other women closer to God. During the two years I led WILL POWER classes, we had three hundred different women come through our door, many of whom did not know of God's love expressed through the gift of His Son. As the classes grew from one a week to eventually ten a week, I needed competent leaders for each of those classes. Some of those wonderful WILL POWER leaders became special friends. One in particular, Pam Dennison, came to work for me as my National Coordinator! Today I'm thankful for the valuable lessons and lifelong friendships I found in WILL POWER.

What's Wrong with This Picture?

Here's what was *wrong* with WILL POWER, and most of the Christian diet groups of recent years:

1. We promoted the lie that thin equals righteousness.
2. We heaped additional guilt upon women who felt plenty guilty already.
3. We baptized all these efforts as dieting "unto-the-Lord."

It simply was not Biblical! Our twelve week format meant many women kept signing up again and again, getting more discouraged. Didn't God want them thin? Why wasn't He being more helpful? It just compounded their problem. Now they had to lose weight not only for themselves and their loved ones, but for God too. I was convinced that (this sounds ridiculous in print) every Christian woman who was overweight was disobedient. She was playing Spiritual Jeopardy, and was doomed to lose the game. Oh, I was quite the finger-shaker. The old, "If I can do it, they can do it," kind of thing.

Carole Shaw, founder of *BBW* magazine, made this observation: "If you're a creep at a size 20, you're a creep at a size 9."[3] That's the truth, and we know it. Then why do we let folks tell us "if you're a creep at a size 20, it's just because you are a 20. Diet your way to a size 10 again, and you'll love yourself more . . . and God will, too!" Ugh.

We can be very hard on ourselves about this issue. Even *People* magazine had a January 1992 cover story entitled "Diet Wars: Who's Winning, Who's Sinning." Featured on the cover? Oprah Winfrey, Liz Taylor and Delta Burke. "Sinners," I suppose. The article also featured Roseanne Arnold and Dolly Parton, among others, and closed with these words: "In our society, is there such a thing as fat and happy?"[4]

Excuse me while I shout: "YES!"

Those of us who are concerned about righteousness (as opposed to *self*-righteousness), often take to heart the suggestion that being overweight is sinful. Among our surveys was this comment:

> *Try to convince me I'm not a fat ugly slob. I struggle spiritually with this . . . gluttony is listed in the Word as a sin . . . I can't seem to 'mortify' this as instructed in Romans 8:13.*
> Sandy from Pennsylvania

Oh, dear friend from my home state! You are not a "fat ugly slob!" You might simply be a large woman. Is that so awful? Words like "big" and "large" can mean very positive things: powerful, mighty, generous, magnificent, spacious, vast, towering, impressive, boundless, substantial, stately and great!

As to her spiritual struggle, I have looked through all the Bible translations I have on hand, and I find there are lots of references to "appetite." However, many times it is not referring to just food, but all the fleshly desires. And those appetites can be found in thin people too.

What the Bible does speak against is overeating to the point of being unable to function or drinking until one is drunk. In Proverbs, it says:

> Do not mix with winebibbers,
> Or with gluttonous eaters of meat;
> For the drunkard and the glutton will come to poverty,
> And drowsiness will clothe a man with rags.[5]

Sinful to be fat? I don't think so. This verse is speaking to the practical, not the spiritual. If you are too "drunk" with wine or food, it *is* hard to function. Sort of how we feel after Thanksgiving dinner, when we really have eaten too much and want to lie on the couch all day! Both the Great Physician and the doctor of the 90's would agree: "all things in moderation." As we've said again and again, being large does not mean you are a glutton. Some of us overeat, some don't. An athlete who eats 5,000 calories a day is not a glutton, because that person's body will burn every one of those calories. It is not how much you eat, but what you do with your body that matters.

What Does God Think About Fat?

There are more than ninety references to "fat" in the Bible, but most of them refer to fat offerings burned unto the Lord. You may remember Abel, of Cain and Abel fame, whose fat offering found favor with the Lord. Also in Genesis is the story of the "sleek, fat cows" versus the "lean, ugly cows." Don't you love that wording? (If anyone ever has the audacity to call you a "fat cow," smile and thank them for knowing beauty when they see it.)

When you think of fat people in Scripture, the name of Eglon, King of Moab may come to mind. After all, right there in Judges 3 it says, "Now Eglon was a very fat man." He was stabbed by Ehud, whose knife disappeared into Eglon's ample belly "and the fat closed over the blade." One dead Eglon. He was the first of 10,000 Moabite men killed by the Israelites. By no means was this king killed because he was fat, nor his men because they were "all stout men of valor." They were oppressing God's people and simply had to go.

The prophet Isaiah spoke of the time when "the glory of Jacob will wane and the fatness of his flesh grow lean." They were not into skinny in those days, because, it seems to me, it would've been downright dangerous. One never knew when a drought or famine might appear on the horizon, so it paid to have some flesh on your bones.

I looked everywhere in Scripture to find an example where fleshiness itself was a problem. Certainly we never hear about anyone's dress size. What size did Ruth wear? Her very name means "beauty," but her size and shape are not mentioned. Her character, on the other hand, is discussed at length. The woman at the well... a size 14? A size 10? Maybe a 22? Who knows? Who cares? The question is: what did she *do* with her life and how did she honor God?

Matthew recorded in his gospel account these words of Jesus:

> The Son of Man came eating and drinking, and they say, "Look, a glutton and a winebibber, a friend of tax collectors and sinners!" But wisdom is justified by her children.[6]

I love this passage because it illustrates perfectly the same kind of hassle we deal with today: People see us eating dessert in a restaurant and jump to the conclusion that we are gluttons or, as we say in the 90's, compulsive overeaters! Jesus was doing nothing wrong, but because He was "different," because people didn't like His message of truth, they looked for something negative to say: "He eats too much, drinks too much, and hangs out with the wrong crowd!"

The last line is the kicker: "But wisdom is justified by her children." Look at the fruit that Jesus' wise choice of companions produced: He gathered together twelve disciples, frankly a bunch of misfits, who changed the world by obeying His commands. (Just for the record, the sizes of their tunics do not appear in any verse.)

The Things That Matter Most

I am not in any way diminishing the spiritual struggles some of us have concerning weight. Having worked through both sides of that issue, I'm here to say without a doubt that the Lord cares a great deal about who we *are* and very little about what we look like.

> For the LORD does not see as man sees; for man looks at the outward appearance, but the LORD looks at the heart.[7]

The number of verses on those two subjects — the body and the heart — is living testimony to which one matters most to God. You'll find a half dozen references to "sleek and fat" (but most of the time the writer was talking about cows!). The character issues, lifestyle issues, how-you-spend-your-days issues, the stuff that really matters — these are discussed a lot more than a handful of times. God cares so much about "love" it shows up more than five hundred times. He wants us to have His "joy," and He talks about it more than two hundred times. "Peace" flows like a river through the Bible another couple hundred different times.

But, Weight Watchers? Not in there, nor any other "Lose Ten Pounds in Ten Days" scheme. Yes, fasting *is* in Scripture, not for the purpose of dieting, but for devotion. No aerobics in the wilderness, no diet aids in the desert, no rocks springing forth with Ultra Slim Fast.

Even Queen Esther, whose beauty carried her to an earthly throne, spent "six months with oil of myrrh, and six months with perfumes and preparations for beautifying women."[8] But nowhere does it say, "And she did two hundred leg lifts every morning, and a thousand sit-ups at night!"

In fact, when you look up all those who "wasted away" in Scripture, you find out pretty quickly that losing weight usually indicated death was right around the corner. So, all my sisters in Christ and especially those whom I unintentionally misinformed during my WILL POWER days: please forgive me and accept God's complete and unconditional love for you. Enter into the joy of your Master, and accept His peace!

Positively the Pits

Let's be honest about something.

There's not a woman alive, including me, who can sail through every minute with a totally optimistic attitude, filled with love, joy and peace. That is just not reality. Even Lizzie, your advocate, the woman who finally found peace at the far end of the dress rack—even I sink deep into the pit again from time to time.

Here's one of my journal entries from one very bad day in August 1992 (yes, a full ten years after I gave my life to God):

> I am sick of being fat.
> I am sick of thinking about it,
> tired of speaking about it. I don't want to write about it.
> I am in pain and denial.
> I don't know how to change.
> I don't want to ask for help.
>
> Look at all these negatives, Lord!
> What happened to Lizzie?
> Why won't this hurt go away?
>
> I can't seem to find a "cause" for it.
> A decision of the will to MAKE it go away
> seems very temporary.
>
> One day I think, "Terrific! I can embrace my fat self,
> and get on with life!" The next day (next hour?),
> I am feeling awful about who I am, what I look like,
> what I FEEL like.
>
> I'm going for a walk. Don't go away, Lord.
> I need You.

I'm glad every day isn't like *that* day. Being a Christian does not mean that our lives will be perfect, that problems are easily solved, or that we'll be filled with joy twenty-four hours a day. Everybody slips into a funk now and again, but I'm on a mission to make sure we don't live there. Our hope lies not in perfection, but in perseverance.

Besides, however awful you feel, it could be worse; you could be on a diet! David Garner, Ph.D., a specialist in eating disorders, states: "Dieting and weight loss may have negative psychological effects, including depression, anxiety, irritability and social withdrawal (and) profoundly negative effects on self-esteem."[9]

Depending on your particular personality type, you may slide down the emotional scale pretty easily. Relax. Emotions change, but the truth does not. This book is about truth, about forgetting the fables and finding out the facts. This chapter is meant to drive home one very important fact: God loves you exactly as you are!

Looking for Love in All the Wrong Places

When it comes to helping women develop a positive self-image, I have a very definite goal in mind: our daughters. Not just the ones some of us gave birth to, but all young women. When we feel good about who we are, it produces a double harvest: our own positive self-esteem *and* the chance to be a positive role model for young women who cross our paths. Unfortunately, we can also offer them a discouraging word.

> *My mother (who is a size 8) says, "You would be so much happier if you were thin."*
>
> Barbara from Ohio

Here is how dangerous I believe low self-esteem is for a young woman. I will attest, absolutely, that negative feelings about her body will drive her to go to extreme lengths to be affirmed by someone. Her mother nags her to go on a diet. Her tiny friends live on 600 calories a day and whine about their flabby thighs. Who will tell this young girl that she's attractive?

Her boyfriend.

What will she do to express her gratitude for his attention? You guessed it.

I'm not speaking to you as a psychologist, a Ph.D., or a certified anything. I am speaking to you as a woman who still has a hard time addressing this subject, but believes it simply must be done. In my heart, I know that if you've made it with me to Chapter Eight, then you're ready to hear what I'm about to share with you.

I had my first sexual experience when I was 16. It was his idea, but I'd read *Everything You Ever Wanted to Know About Sex (but were afraid to ask)*, so I thought I was ready. I remember crying afterward and feeling like I had ruined my life for something that wasn't even fun.

Why did I, a woman from a good family, stray from my parents' teachings? I wasn't overwhelmed with passion, or even curiosity. I just wanted somebody to tell me I was pretty.

I soon discovered that boys were very interested in a girl who would "let them," so I just let them. One after another. I counted for a long time, then gave up at well over two hundred. I decided sex was one thing I could excel in, something exciting and dangerous. It made me feel wanted, part of life, even if I knew deep down that it was sleazy and awful and the men didn't care a thing about me.

Oh, how I tried to please them! I hoped that then they would tell me what I wanted to hear: "Liz, you are desirable! You are beautiful! You are wanted!"

I don't know if every woman who grew up struggling with her body image found solace in the arms of appreciative men, but this woman did.

The opposite sex wasn't the only place I looked for acceptance and escape from my pain. By the time I went to college, I was experimenting with drugs. Just pot and hash and pills, no LSD, no acid. This wasn't because I was choosy, but only because, thank goodness, I never ran into any of those particular drugs at a party. Otherwise, I would have tried them, no questions asked.

By my early 20's, I'd found a new friend that was 100 proof. I began drinking regularly. It felt so good to just slip away, to feel so loose and carefree. At my first college frat party, I drank nineteen beers, one for each of my nineteen years. Eventually I passed out, and someone rolled me under a picnic table just so I wouldn't get stepped on.

Blackouts were to become a more common occurrence as the years went by. Some weekends I'd wake up at noon in some stranger's apartment in another city, and I'd have to ask them to drive me home.

It seems unbelievable now, but it was the life I considered normal then. About the only thing that was normal (i.e., acceptable) during this period was my weight. I had gradually dieted myself down to 135, and I stayed there simply because I had only seven dollars a week to spend on groceries. The rest was spent on clothes, pot and bar-hopping.

Shopping was another means of affirming my worth, and a legal "high." Through my mid-20's, I owned twelve credit cards, all run up to the maximum limit and then some. Clothes shopping, especially while stoned, was a favorite pastime, even after my weight had climbed to pre-diet limits. The clerks would giggle at my dazed expression. But I just had them put all those nice size 16 outfits on hangers, and I drifted out into the mall.

When the radio station I was working for suddenly changed format, I took the first available job and headed for my present home in Louisville. Cocaine wasn't as available in this smaller city, but the homegrown pot was cheap and effective. I spent every evening the same way: a joint to relax me, then a drink of Southern Comfort and soda to keep me mellow for six hours in front of the tube.

I seriously contemplated suicide one sunny afternoon after a terrible day at work when I'd screamed at everyone within earshot. But I couldn't think of a method of killing myself that wouldn't hurt. Thanks to my basic fear of pain, and thanks to Tim and Ev Kelly, I'm alive.

A Change of Heart

Tim and Ev came into my life in the fall of 1981. They were a dynamic radio duo who moved to Louisville to do the morning show at my station. I loved them immediately, because they had everything I ever wanted: looks, talent, money, professional credentials, a house in the country, a beautiful daughter and a Mercedes (well, it was leased, but it was nice!). The only thing I wasn't too crazy about was the fact that they called themselves Christians. Ugh. I'd been around enough church people in my life to be wary. They didn't talk about church, though. They talked about Jesus — like they knew Him. More important to me at the time, they loved me, accepted me, invited me into their home, fed me Thanksgiving dinner, and didn't judge me for the life I led. When I would light up a joint, they'd start talking about a "better way."

"A better high?" I said, with interest.

"Yes, sort of," they assured me. "And you'll never have a hangover!"

When they finally did invite me to church, I was ready to find out if there were any other people as warm and weird and wonderful as these two.

There were. Pews full of them!

It didn't take me long to realize that here was the source of love that I had been searching for. God, my creator, who knew me and loved me completely, had been waiting for me all along. On those days when my mirror said "Ugh!" God said, "Ahh!" Hallelujah! Shalom!

The changes in my life, thanks to this new spiritual dimension, were amazing. I unplugged my television for a season and started reading the Bible and singing in the choir. I let the booze and pot run out and never felt the need to replace them. A nice enough young man that I was dating (and sleeping with) was sent on his merry way, and I cut the credit cards up into dozens of tiny pieces.

As you've already read, then I did the WILL POWER number. Down the scale for a two-year stint at thin, then up again for good. We're talking major self-esteem collapse at this point, because I'd put the cart before the horse by believing the fable: "Lose weight, and you'll love yourself more." Wrong! If anything, the reverse might be true: If you love yourself more, you might (accidentally, of course) lose weight. Or you might not lose weight. But either way, you end up loving yourself.

Judy Simon, M.S., is a registered dietitian from Michigan, with a slim body but a sympathetic heart. In her presentation, "Women's Struggle with Body Image," she made this statement:

> Body image is quite independent of physical characteristics. Changing your body itself does not improve your body image or your self-esteem. [But] changing your body image by accepting yourself allows you to increase your self-esteem and make changes in your physical appearance in a healthy and loving manner.[10]

Or, I might add, *not* make changes in your physical appearance, depending on your body's needs. For some of us, it was the heart changes that made the biggest difference of all.

You Took the Words Right Out of My Mouth!

From 1984 to 1986, I lost all that supposed willpower, and gained back all my lost weight and much more. I was very embarrassed about the whole thing. I avoided eye contact with my former students, though many of them were gaining too. I couldn't bear the public scrutiny.

I remember getting a phone call one very down day from a woman in a nearby city. She began the call somewhat hesitantly, and addressed me by my maiden name. Certain it was some telemarketing person, I snapped back at her, "Ma'am, I've been married for several years, and my name is no longer Amidon!"

"Oh!" she was stammering now. "I've been trying to track you down for a long time. I belong to a church here in Lexington, and I wanted to know more about your WILL POWER program."

I felt something go "zing" in my chest as I almost shouted, "WILL POWER? There is no such thing! It doesn't work! It never did! Tell the women of your church to stop dieting and start living!"

Long silence. "Okay," she said. More silence. "Well, thank you very much for your time. I'm sorry that I bothered you, Liz." I mumbled something, then hung up the phone. To say I didn't handle that opportunity to encourage her is the understatement of a lifetime. Lord, forgive me when I have my foot so firmly planted between my teeth I can't talk right.

My overreaction to her request was just another indication that my self-esteem, and self-control, had hit rock bottom. That's what it took for me to get to the truth. My worth could not be measured by any scale, any bank account, any dress size, anything other than my complete acceptance of God's love, Bill's love, my children's love, unconditional love. Do I wish I had never gained back all those pounds? Not this woman. What I have gained in understanding, humility (sometimes!), and compassion is worth every inch.

The fun part is, all across America other women are making the same discovery: self-worth is of much greater value than net worth:

> *Since I hold little hope of ever becoming "slim et trim," I look for encouragement to help me stay positive. The Lord created us — creatures great (big) and small. I'm okay with that, and I love and serve the Lord just as well as any skinny person could.*
> Glenna from Illinois

If we've moved forward on the path to self-acceptance, gained some understanding of why we think, feel and act the way we do, and given up on "perfect" then we're ready for the next step: *being* perfected, which means "completed, finished." It's a process, not a place or destination.

Getting my "insides" right helps me accept my outside self too. Body confidence is a product of self-confidence, which is a product of spiritual confidence in the One who loves me even if I never lose an ounce. That's why they call it "Amazing Grace."

Begin Building Body Confidence Today

1. Write a working definition of self-esteem in twenty words or less. Choose your words carefully. Craft this definition to best meet your needs. Let it be both a statement of where you are now and where you're going. Put it where you'll see it today and every day.

2. Start a journal. Any old notebook will do, or type it into the computer like I do. Don't make it a "have to" thing, another daily grind. Let it be a place where your innermost thoughts can be recorded for your eyes only. Sometimes you may need to share them with someone, as I have shared some of my deep, dark stuff with you. If someone is willing to listen, it can be very freeing for you.

3. Make a list of the places that you have looked for attention, affection and affirmation. Did they consistently provide that? Do you believe God might fill that need for you?

❤ A Fashion Magazine Editor Speaks . . .

Carole Shaw is the founder of *BBW: Big Beautiful Woman* magazine, the first and only fashion magazine for the large size woman.

Liz: How did *BBW* happen?

Carole: *It was 1978, and I had suddenly realized after thirty years of dieting that I had gained fifty pounds. [Laughing] I decided right then that I wasn't going to diet anymore. Instead of buying temporary clothes, I went off with a fistful of cash to buy real clothes. Was I disappointed! The selection was awful . . . bullet-proof polyester pants and maternity tops. Ugh. I came home crying. What options did I have? Diet again? No way. Go through my life in fat lady clothes? No thanks. My husband said, "Stop crying and do something!" "Okay!" I said. "I'll do a magazine for big women!" To this day, I don't know where that thought came from. A few days later, he said, "Let's do the magazine!" "How?" I asked. "You'll think of something," he said.*

Liz: So you two were in on this thing together from the beginning.

Carole: *And we're still a team today. We broke all the fat lady fashion rules. We took the clothes that were available at the time —polyester pantsuits, mostly —and did the unthinkable. We belted them! Of course, there were no belts to be found, so we used curtain ties. We tucked in blouses, we used colors other than black. And our models, all of whom were size 16 or larger, wore lovely makeup and hairstyles, which was a no-no. Big women were supposed to be invisible.*

Liz: You went national with the second issue of *BBW*. What really made it take off?

Carole: *I did a half-hour with Tom Snyder on the old* Tomorrow *show. At the end, he gave me a big kiss. That kiss easily got us 7,000 subscriptions.*

Liz: Did you do any test marketing for this concept?

Carole: *None. I had lived in this body for many years, and I knew what hurt my feelings. What I needed and what drove me crazy was the same for* BBW's *all over the country. It was all instinct. And it worked. We just celebrated fourteen years in print, and we now publish 200,000 copies per issue.*

Liz: Your background was not in journalism, but in show business.

Carole: *That's right. I was a performer, a singer. My hit record was on the Verve label, called "Careless." I was travelling, doing shows all over the country—radio, television, Ed Sullivan, the works. But when I came out of the television studio, I never asked, "How did I sound?" I asked, "Did I look too fat?" I was always on a diet, always agonizing over my weight. Recently, I got to see some of those old TV clips, and I got so angry at myself. I was not fat! My goal with* BBW *magazine is to see that our next generation of young women doesn't waste time and energy dieting and messing up their metabolism.*

Liz: You have two daughters. Are they also big, beautiful women?

Carole: *Beautiful, yes, but they're thin. I like them anyway! We appeared on the Sally Jesse Raphael show together, talking about mothers and daughters and the weight issue. My daughters say they are "fat blind."*

Liz: You have a wonderful sense of humor. How does that fit into your life as a big, beautiful woman?

Carole: *I think anyone who has survived any kind of hardship or challenge in life has to develop a sense of humor about it. I'm not talking about the "jolly fat lady" approach. The ability to see humor in life has no size attached. I use humor as a teaching tool. And, I do THIN jokes!*

Liz: What has been the most satisfying thing about *BBW*?

Carole: *Personal appearances are my favorite because I love watching women change both their attitudes and style of dressing right before my eyes. The "fat lady costume" is gone forever! I also love when I'm sitting in an airport and a woman comes over, hugs me and says, "Thank you." That is very moving for me, and makes all the effort worthwhile.*

Liz: What has been your biggest challenge as editor-in-chief?

Carole: *It has taken some time to win over Madison Avenue. The people who manufacture clothes for the larger woman love us, of course, but those who make other products for women — shampoo, cosmetics, and the like — seem to hesitate about buying advertising in* BBW, *for fear women might think they'll gain weight if they use that product! It's silly. I tell them, once the dollars are in the till, you can't tell the fat money from the thin money.*

Liz: What areas in the fashion industry still need to wake up to this underserved population?

Carole: *Big, beautiful teens need clothes just like their contemporaries, and those are still hard to come by. Supersize women, women over size 24, need more options. And maternity clothes for the larger woman are awful!*

Liz: How well I remember! You are doing some things to improve our options, with *BBW* Pattern Collection for Simplicity up to size 32, with your own book, *Big Beautiful Woman: Come Out, Come Out, Wherever You Are!*, even with your own perfume, "Confidence!"

Carole: *It has been an incredible experience — exciting and fun and humbling all at the same time. I would urge every woman of any size to give herself permission to be happy and successful!*

"Big People Are Always Jolly" (Ha!)

One day, I was having my upstairs bedroom wallpapered. There is a floor heating vent in that room, and after the men left, my mother said, "I'm going to clean out that vent. Be careful, I have the top grate off."

Minutes later, I walked into the bedroom with an armload of laundry. The men had left newspapers all over the floor, and a screwdriver was hidden underneath them. Guess who stepped on it, went flying into the air and down into the vent?!

My legs were hanging through the downstairs ceiling, my arms and head were in the upstairs bedroom and I couldn't move. My mother, scared to death, kept yelling, "Be careful, or you'll fall through!" I told her, "No way! I'm stuck — and as soon as I can stop laughing, I'll try to get out and pick the splinters out of my tail!"

Betty from Kentucky

I love that story. Such experiences for us big women can either be hysterically funny or just hysterical. It's all in how you look at things.

*It's always an encouragement to know that I'm not alone. Many
women struggle with their size. It'll be nice to laugh about it, even
though the tears are always hiding behind my laughter.*
                                        Rosanna from Kentucky

I have both laughed until I cried, and cried so much that I finally
started laughing again. My dear friend and a consummate speaking
professional, Rosita Perez, says, "Laughter comes from a very deep
need not to cry." From her years in social work, she learned firsthand
how people use laughter as a coping mechanism. After all, there are
much worse ways to handle pain! Drugs, alcohol, violence — those
are the negative means of dealing with life's indignities.

Laughter, on the other hand, offers some of the same qualities: it
is addictive and habit-forming: it gives us a "high"; it's a release for
pent-up emotions; and, it can be noisy and disruptive. The big
differences are: laughter is good for your body, mind and spirit, it
hurts no one, and it entertains everyone within earshot. Not bad, for
free!

Don't Make Me Laugh!

Some of us have been so afraid of the "jolly fat person" stereotype
that we've tried to prove just how serious we can be. In the process,
we may be missing the wonderful release of pain, anger and frustration
that laughter provides.

*Humor is important. I'm not interested in an "us versus them"
attitude, rather in something that helps me feel like a valid member
of humanity and helps me laugh at my own foolish attitudes and
those of others . . . while recognizing I'm different, the point is that
we're more the same.*
                                        Mary Jane from Kentucky

Humor is the great leveling agent. It pulls down the haughty and
picks up the humble. People all over the world love to laugh. It's one
of the qualities we humans have that separates us from the beasts. It
is, along with music, one of God's most generous gifts to His creation.

Henri Bergson said, "Laughter needs an echo." We do like to
laugh *with* someone. As a means of communication, it is the purest,
most honest, trusting expression of ourselves we could give one

another. When you've laughed wholeheartedly with someone, you've been completely yourself. As you probably found out one Halloween, you can't laugh with a mask on!

I had some nifty refrigerator magnets made up with these words from Konrad Lorenz: "Heartily laughing together at the same thing forms an immediate bond." So true! When we've shared a big laugh together, some invisible walls have come down between us, and we've taken our relationship one step higher.

A Flight of Fancy

Comedians always begin, "Have you heard the one about...?" Well, I know you haven't heard this one, because only two women in the world know it happened. (When you finish reading this, there will be three of us!).

I had just walked into the passenger terminal at the Indianapolis airport and was looking for somewhere to land until they called my flight. Almost every seat was filled. At the end of one of the rows were two seats joined together on a T-shaped base. On one of those seats sat a very thin young lady who barely took up half of her side. "Perfect!" I thought, heading toward the other vacant side.

I sat down carefully, smiled at her, and began to arrange my packages around me. As I was leaning over to close my briefcase, this little slip of a woman apparently stood up. Unfortunately, she was my ballast.

Seconds later, I was shouting out something like, "G-r-r-a-a-a-a-k-k!" I turned the entire double seat completely over sideways and I went tumbling, tails over teacups. Needless to say, this attracted the attention of the men at the ticket counter, who rushed over to help.

They couldn't get me off the floor. Not because of my size (after all, there were three of them), not because I was pinned under the chair, but because I was laughing too hard. All my muscles were so relaxed I was like a large, limp Raggedy Ann doll on roller skates.

They kept asking me, "Are you okay, Miss? Are you okay? Shall we call a doctor?" Well, that just made me laugh harder, until I was almost gasping for air. Finally, they helped me get to a standing position and steered me toward the seat, back on its T-shaped feet again. I very carefully sat down in the middle of the T and took a deep breath.

Assuring everyone around me that I was just fine, I began to pull my coat together and stuff some things back into my carry-on bag.

Every few seconds, I had to stifle another giggle. Pulling out a small mirror to check and see if my lipstick had survived my unscheduled "flight," I caught a glimpse of another large woman seated near me who was watching me with great interest. Her lips were so tightly pinched together, she looked like she had swallowed a large cat.

I sized her up as a "sister" immediately, leaned over to her and whispered, "I'm just thankful I didn't flip that little woman up in the air."

That was all it took. This woman exploded with the loudest "H-a-a-a-w-w-w-w!" I've ever heard, before or since. Having just barely recovered myself, I was right in there with her, howling and snorting and slapping my knee. People would not even look in our direction.

I may never see her again, but that woman and I are now joined at the funny bone for life!

Humor That Heals

Every now and then, a woman attending one of my presentations will slip a note in my hand before she slips out the door. Others will drop a letter in the mail later. Such correspondence is always precious to me. This one in particular, from a woman in Wisconsin, was especially touching:

> *I am a size twenty-four, and have always felt that I had to hide except in coming to work. I am forty-seven and have hidden within my fat, dying to escape into the fun world to do all that I think I cannot because of my size. You showed me such insight into having a good time, by laughing and being sure of yourself and all a mere size twenty-two . . . I just cannot begin to tell you the impact you had on me.*

What a blessing, and how humbling, to be in the right place at the right time for this woman. In sharing so honestly with me (and now, anonymously, with you), she has given us a great gift: herself.

Rosita Perez says, "The older we get, and the more comfortable we get with ourselves, the easier it is to laugh. I once was speaking and looked down to discover a run in my stocking. I told the audience, 'Fifteen years ago, this run would have ruined my day. Isn't it wonderful that today, it doesn't really matter?'"

I have gained more than just a dress size or two these last few years. I have gained quite a bit of knowledge about the subjects of dieting and humor, plus a few insights about myself. Here is the summary of all I have learned:

> Fat, miserable women go on diets and cry.
> Big, bountiful women eat intelligently and LAUGH!

Each day I ask myself, "Liz, to which do you aspire?" I like the second approach better.

False Advertising

I once ordered a book with a most promising title, *Laugh It Off.* It was billed as the "new humor strategy of weight loss," and since I love to laugh and love to hear the latest theories about weight loss, comical and otherwise, I ordered it. By page four, I was not a happy reader. The author insisted: "FAT brings me ILL health, ILL feelings, an ILL nature and ILLusions."[1]

Later she states, "The human body is made to THIN specifications." Oh, is that a fact? Has God shown her His blueprint for humankind? One glance around our globe makes it pretty clear that small is not all there is! What I thought would be, at the very least, a fun book was in fact yet another dreary, All-Fat-People-Are-Compulsive-Overeaters book. Ugh.

To genuinely "lighten up" doesn't mean weighing less on the scale, but having a lighter heart. What is usually lifted from our hearts is pain. My best humor comes out of pain, because it's at that heartfelt level I connect with my audience. Our century's greatest clown, Red Skelton, said: "No matter what your heartache may be, laughing helps you forget it for a few seconds."

The rules are clear on this: I can turn my own pain into humor, but I cannot and should not turn *your* pain into humor. The first is funny, the second is sick and usually passes as R-rated comedy. As Nancy Loving said, "The richest laugh is at no one's expense."

Finding Humor at Every Turn

I write all my own humor, most of it based on real-life stuff from my diary. When I began speaking full-time in 1987, I was constantly shopping for stories to build my repertoire, looking for humor in all the off-the-wall things that happened in our little honeymoon household.

Bill would cringe every time he did something that made me laugh, and say, "Don't tell me that's going to end up in your speech Friday night!" If he really meant it, of course I didn't include it. Now, several years and two kids later, the situation has changed drastically.

These days Bill comes home from work, saying, "Oh, I did this really goofy thing today. Do you want to hear about it? Maybe you could use it in your next speech." I think my hubby has decided he likes being the star of my stories.

In her book, *Sizing Up*, author Sandy Summers Head lists the six qualities that beautiful women of all sizes, from all over the world, seem to share:

- Acceptance
- Sensuality
- Health
- Grooming
- Style
- Sense of Humor[2]

Although there are some parts of her book that I'm not thrilled with (too much dieting advice), in this analysis she is right on target. These are all qualities that every woman can pursue regardless of weight, body type, age, color, or any other characteristic. The easiest one to work on (and the one that won't cost you a dime) is your sense of humor.

> *I'm always working on improving myself by understanding who I am — then not taking myself so seriously and DEVELOPING MY SENSE OF HUMOR!*
>
> Cindy from Kentucky

A sense of humor is like any other sense: with time and effort, it can be developed. For example, you can't improve your hearing, but you can improve your listening skills. In the same way, you can't really learn to be funny, but you can learn to recognize and utilize humor. Usually those of us who value humor have found some way to keep it ever-handy when we need it.

We've all enjoyed those "office handouts," as I call them. It's that stuff that shows up at the copy machine one day and soon every part of the building has a copy of it posted on the bulletin board. More than once, a handout has centered around dieting. Alas, these things never list authors or sources or references or copyrights, so I'll have to give credit for this one to the Great Copy Machine in the Sky. It was labeled, "The Rules of Dieting," and featured, among some old standbys, this new favorite: "Cookie pieces contain no calories, because the process of breaking them causes calorie leakage." A classic.

I'll bet you've seen one of those ubiquitous greeting cards with the little lamb on it that says, "Ewes not fat, ewes just fluffy." Is this supposed to make me feel better? Sheep are not too bright, don't smell very nice, get lost easily and have almost no initiative whatsoever. They get fleeced annually and end up as lamb chops! I'll stick with being fat.

A Big Sense of Humor

So what does it mean to be a large and funny woman? Are we all Roseanne Arnold? No. Truly funny people aren't stereotypes at all, nor are they copycats. They're original. Off beat. Dabbling in the unexpected. Above all, they have to be confident in their ability to communicate their view of the world in such a way that others see the humor in it too.

> *Give a chuckle now and then. Life is heavy enough just being heavy weight-wise. But upbeat doesn't have to be Richard Simmons — a person can be positive without always flying two feet off the ground!*
>
> Linda from California

(Armadillos fly two feet off the ground when they are startled by the oncoming lights of an automobile, and look where it gets *them*!)

We all need more humor in our lives (especially those who are "lean and mean"). Everybody needs to laugh. We need to laugh at our bizarre bodies, our funny experiences, our strange little personality quirks, our odd idiosyncracies, the ill-harbored anxieties we barely contain. Whatever will connect us to other human beings, that's going to be our best source of humor.

> *I need to be able to laugh at my size (more). To be more candid about it (like you). Give me inspiration on days when I need it.*
>
> Marcia from South Dakota

Laughter can be used to cover up *or* to disclose our true selves.

Eye to Eye, Heart to Heart

If you haven't already, you'll meet humorist Jeanne Robertson at the end of this chapter, a T-A-L-L woman with an even taller sense of humor. She has turned her unusual physical characteristic — being 6'2" (make that 5'14") in her stocking feet — into a hilarious platform for her humor. Her height is not all she speaks about, by any means. It just gives her a good launching pad, a way to connect with her audience.

Although everyone may not be 6'2", everyone does have something different about them that they can't change and need to accept, even laugh about. Jeanne helps them do that by leading the way. As Gail from Kentucky says, "[I need] humor and words of wisdom from successful women in all walks of life who know that size is a very small part of a total person."

Our size is a small part of who we are. It just happens to be the part people see first. But once they've fully processed that fact, I believe our size becomes much less of an issue.

A Sense of Humor, A Sense of Self

During the opening moments of my program, I almost always have a little fun with my size. After all, it's the thing an audience is likely to notice first about me, so I address it up front in a humorous way.

I have two reasons for doing this. One is to help people relax and start laughing. They always look sort of relieved, as if to say, "Oh, she *knows* she's big!" I'm also giving them permission to laugh at themselves a little, to see their own differences and celebrate them.

I often tell them about the letter I received from a group of prisoners during my radio years. They wrote:

Dear Lizzie:

The guys in Cell Block D have taken a bet on what you look like. We think you have olive skin, long, dark straight hair, that you're about 5'2" and weigh 105 pounds. Are we close?

Your friends at
Kentucky State Reformatory

So I wrote them back and said, "Gosh, fellas, I can't believe how . . . CLOSE you were!" (I hope they're in for fifteen years-to-life.)

Ethel Barrymore said, "You grow up the day you have your first real laugh — at yourself." I've been laughing at myself for decades, and I've learned I'm not alone:

> *I usually say to people, "I used to have a dynamite figure. Then, I exploded." That puts them at ease and we all laugh and get on with things.*
>
> Dorothy from Kentucky

Sometimes such humor is called "self-deprecating." I agree with Jeanne Robertson, who says, "I don't like the term 'put-down' humor or 'self-deprecating humor.' I see it as a humor born of self-confidence and self-acceptance." Rosita Perez echoes that, saying a woman who can laugh at herself is "intelligent, confident, at ease with herself, contemplative. She can dissect her life, then come up with something that's shareable."

I'll often say during a presentation, "I'm a big, beautiful woman in a narrow, nervous world." The audience always responds positively, because it is obvious from my word choices that I feel good about who I am ("beautiful") and sorry for others ("narrow," "nervous") who were not as abundantly created.

The voluptuous Mae West, who always looked like she was poured into her dress and forgot to say "when," was famous for stating," Too much of a good thing can be wonderful."

> *The best one [I've heard] so far is "You are horizontally gifted."*
>
> Nancy from Wisconsin

Another comment along those lines is "gravitationally challenged!" The key is, it's perfectly permissible for us to laugh at ourselves in any fashion we're comfortable with. What's not appropriate is others making comments about our size. The first indicates self-acceptance; the second suggests insensitivity.

Stepping Over the Line

Not all fat people are the happy, jolly, always funny people. We also have emotions and fat jokes hurt our feelings just like everyone else.

Connie from Wisconsin

There is a very fine line between having a little fun with your size, and overdoing such humor. I've crossed the line myself more than once, and the audience always lets me know in a very simple way: They stop laughing. In their eyes, I've moved from self-acceptance to self-effacement. Instead of being happy for me, they feel sorry for me. It's critical for all of us who use humor in any form, to understand the difference and stay on the right side of this line.

I may use what Carole Shaw calls "thin jokes!" Without speaking unkindly about those who are smaller, it's possible to offer a gentle jab in their general direction. When I speak of my daughter Lillian, I say, "I don't know whether Lillian will grow up to be built like her mother or not, but I've promised God that if she's thin, I'll still love her." No one is the butt of this joke, and everyone laughs at it. Another good example of this kind of humor comes from Kathryn Grayson, who said: "The worst kind of reducing pill is the one who keeps telling you how she did it."

Humor about ourselves is a female phenomenon. Psychologist Judith Tingley notes that women like humor of such a personal nature, but men don't. Men often respond to more hostile jokes about "the other guy," and women do not. We'd rather laugh at ourselves and our own foibles.

For example, if I'm speaking to a mixed audience, I might poke a little fun at some fellow's tie, along the lines of "Did your wife pick that one out for you? Oh, you picked it out? That explains it." Everyone laughs at this kind of thing, including the man wearing the tie. The truth is, he probably loves being the center of attention. But, to reverse the roles, I would never in a million years choose a woman out of the audience and say, "Will you look at that skirt? Where did you get such an ugly thing?" The audience would be appalled, she would be mortified, and I would soon be looking for another profession. It's just not done.

Can I explain this male/female difference? Nope. It's just a social reality. We women feel more comfortable laughing at ourselves, and feel equally at ease with another woman who's doing the same thing. One study of male and female comics found that 63% of the comediennes included self-disparaging comments, while only 12% of male comics did so.[3]

Humorist Hope Mihalap, a Greek woman who is married to a Russian professor and lives in the South (you can see where she finds her material!), thinks that when a woman has a little fun at her own expense, it "denotes a little more security. She knows that she is loved, and is confident that people love her for who she is. Therefore, she has the freedom to laugh at herself."

In fact, developmental psychologist Dr. Paul E. McGee believes that "self-disparagement may play a unique role in the establishment of a female sense of humor."[4] This is for all women, of course, not just larger women. Tall humorist Jeanne Robertson commented, "Some people say, 'If you woke up short, you'd be nothing.' That's not true. If I woke up short, I'd just write new material."

Most folks who are funny for money are delighted to have some natural material to work with. Watch any stand-up comic, male or female, and they will invariably poke fun at their bald head, big nose, skinny legs, large ears, wide hips, whatever physical characteristic that's obvious to the audience. Then, they'll often switch to humor about their personality or emotional self, or some other unique traits we may not be able to see, but will identify with immediately.

That's really the whole point of using humor: identification. Connecting with one another on some basic level. Laughter tears down walls and builds bridges. How we laugh and what we laugh about reveal a great deal about who we are and how we feel about ourselves. Allen Funt of *Candid Camera* fame, made this observation:

> I think that a sense of humor is deeply involved with a person's self-image. If you like yourself, you have a chance to observe and enjoy situations around you without being threatened or feeling inferior.[5]

The Best Medicine

Not only is laughter important for a healthy self-esteem, it helps us have a healthier body too. One of my favorite programs to present is called, "One Laugh to Live!" It's a 90-minute romp through the latest theories on the health-enhancing, stress-relieving power of humor. Flocks of people always come when this program is offered, which simply means we all yearn to laugh more.

It wasn't *Reader's Digest* who decided that "Laughter is the Best Medicine." Thousands of years ago, Solomon wisely wrote, "A merry heart does good, like medicine."[6]

Did you know, for example, that a big, hearty laugh actually raises your heart rate a bit, then drops it below the starting level? True! Laughing has the same effect on blood pressure, elevating it just slightly, then dropping it back to a new, improved level.

Of course, I realize you could accomplish the same two things with exercise. Theoretically. I always like to follow the advice of comedy writer Robert Orben, who cautions, "The important thing to remember about exercise is to start slow, and then gradually taper off."

Here's another body benefit: laughing massages your organs. Things like your kidneys, pancreas, and spleen. I mean really, have you thought about your spleen lately? It's been thinking of you, saying, "Boy, I could use a good workout." Laughing hard does just that. Norman Cousins called it "internal jogging."

Fifteen facial muscles get into the act when you let loose with a big laugh. If you've ever laughed so hard your cheeks hurt, that's why! Your sore cheeks are trying to tell you, "Please do this more than once a year." Laughing hard also oxygenates the body. In order to laugh out, you have to take air in, and that oxygen exchange is vital. In fact, with a big laugh, you can exhale up to seventy-five miles per hour (which suggests it might be a good idea not to sit in front of somebody with false teeth!).

Josh Billings said it best: "There ain't much fun in medicine, but there's a heck of a lot of medicine in fun!"

Stress Buster

The greatest benefit of laughter for many of us is its ability to help us handle stress. My friend Dr. Clifford Kuhn of the University of Louisville, a psychiatrist and a stand-up comic, says, "Humor won't cure anything, but it does improve a person's resources for dealing with the stresses of life."

Stress really is the disease of this decade. For me, the most stressful privilege I undertake each day is mothering my two precious children. The neat thing is that, although kids may add a little stress to your life, they also bring with them an antidote for stress: they laugh all the time. Babies laugh on average of four times an hour, and toddlers laugh fifteen times an hour!

Until we get our hands on them: "Don't you laugh at that, young man! You think you're so funny. It is not appropriate to giggle during the sermon!" And so on. Pretty soon, children get the idea that Mother has no sense of humor.

If you were to get a letter from me, you would see at the bottom of my stationery a little quote which I made up. It summarizes my philosophy on this subject: "The head thinks, the hands labor, but it's the heart that laughs."

As I travel all over America, I find women of all sizes who are incredibly good at using their heads. We are so bright we can do anything! We're good at using our hands, too, and are gifted and skilled beyond measure. But sometimes we get so busy using our heads and our hands, we forget to exercise our hearts.

I don't only mean in a cardiovascular sense (though as a volunteer for the American Heart Association, I know that's important too). I mean nurturing yourself at the deepest level of who you are, your emotional, spiritual self. That's the part of you that responds to humor, and that's where a laugh takes place. Something funny travels through your eyes or ears, then on through your brain, but it isn't until it hits your heart that a laugh comes out.

Real laughter is not at all premeditated. Nobody is sitting there saying to themselves, "I think I'll laugh in thirteen seconds." The laughter catches us by surprise, gives our heart a little workout, and chases away stress for a season.

Here's an example of how laughter turned a stressful situation into a happier one. Last spring, I tried on a large, plaid suit. We're talking big plaid, big suit. It was gorgeous, my size exactly and a perfect fit. But when I looked in the mirror, I didn't look so much dressed as I did upholstered. Big covered buttons, the whole routine. Just put a skirt around my ankles and stick me in your living room!

Not only is humor available everywhere, great for your body and good for your soul, it is actually dangerous *not* to laugh. Think of all the pent-up stress clogging your arteries! Think of all those stressed-out muscles trying to keep up your pantyhose. Without question, the woman of the 90's must laugh loud and laugh often, or risk the inevitable. As Fred Allen puts it, "It is bad to suppress laughter. It goes back down and spreads to your hips."

Begin Building Body Confidence Today

1. Think of a funny incident when your size factored into the hilarity of the moment. Write it down, then share it with a friend. (While you're at it, I'd love to read it too! Mail me a copy, and I'll try and include it in a future publication, credited to you.)

2. Begin collecting your favorite humorous anecdotes, cartoons, and one-liners. You might record them in a loose-leaf notebook, a humor journal, whatever suits your style. The key is to have it ready to go when the need for laughter strikes.

3. If you don't already have a quick, clever, put-everyone-at-ease comeback to someone who mentions your size, begin working on such a comment. By having it on hand, you'll relax about such situations a little more and increase your ability to laugh at life and yourself while you chase away stress!

❤ A Humorist Speaks . . .

At 6'2" in her stocking feet, Jeanne Robertson was the tallest woman to ever enter the Miss America contest. (She's happy to point out that she was also the tallest woman to ever lose the Miss America contest!) Since her pageant days in the 60's, Jeanne has entertained audiences all over America with her tall tales and southern-spun humor. A past-president of the National Speakers Association, Jeanne is the author of *Humor: The Magic of Genie*.

Liz: What do people say when they meet you for the first time?

Jeanne: *I was 6'2" at age thirteen, so people have been commenting about my height for most of my life. Let's face it, height and weight are both very noticeable things, and people feel free to make some remark about them when they meet us. When I was young, people always said, "My, how you've grown!" It got to be a joke with my family, such that when we went to visit our relatives in Auburn, my parents would say, "How many times do you think you'll hear, 'My how you've grown'?" We'd even place bets on it. Then, when the comments would come, instead of being embarrassed, I would cut my eyes at my mother and we would nod: "That's one! That's two!" It was funny, and helped me through a very awkward time. Later, they encouraged me to mention it myself, so I'd jump out of the car and say, "My, how I've grown!"*

Liz: Do you think people are intentionally trying to hurt us when they make such comments?

Jeanne: *I really don't. That's why the best response is a humorous one, laughing at yourself, rather than looking for the curt comeback, the one-line zinger. Just recently, I realized that I do something unintentionally that's really very inappropriate. When I'm around a larger man who I know, I'll sometimes poke him in the stomach with my index finger. Of course, it's done in fun, but it's still not right. Unfortunately, we often do such things without really thinking about how it might make the other person feel.*

Liz: What are some of the less funny things, the drawbacks, of being a tall woman?

Jeanne: *The big problem is shopping for clothes. You can't buy anything at the last minute. I've always envied women who can start shopping on Wednesday for a dress they need Saturday night. I have to plan way ahead, and I always have to have things altered. Those of us who are bigger or taller than average almost always spend more money on our wardrobe, and end up with a lot of things we don't wear. If I pass a tall woman coming out of the mall with a big package, my first thought is, "Well, whatever was worth buying, she found it first." If I see a woman in the tall girl store looking through my size, I practically hyperventilate. When I do find something that fits, I always buy it, figuring "I'd better get it today, it may not be here later." I suppose I could find a good tailor, pick out fabrics and so forth, but I'm too busy for all that.*

Liz: It's amazing to me how similar our challenges are in that regard. Now, what are some of the advantages of being tall?

Jeanne: *When you are 6'2", there's no way you won't be noticed when you walk into a room. There is in fact nothing you can do in the way of clothing that will make you not be noticed. Flat shoes look ridiculous with an outfit that calls for heels, so I wear the heels. For the most part, the taller woman looks good in her clothes. She can make a statement, hopefully a positive one. Those of us who are not a "normal" size have a common bond. We can see each other across the room and start grinning, because we know we've had many of the same experiences. Women who are extra large, extra tall, even extra short, all share some of the same challenges. I believe that larger and taller women who develop a high degree of self-confidence command more respect and attention and have more presence about them. I really do think size can be an advantage!*

Liz: Does one size ever fit your all?

Jeanne: *NO! Well, that's not true. I had a One Size Fits All umbrella once that was a good fit.*

Liz: Is the rest of your family tall, too?

Jeanne: *Not my parents or siblings, but my husband is 6'6" and my son is 6'8". One of the challenges of raising a tall teenager is finding clothes that are in style. Yes, you can find him jeans, but not the "in" jeans. An adult may not care about the label thing very much, but it matters a lot to a teenager. I remember the time my son and husband were trying to buy a blouse for me, and the clerk asked what size foundation I wore. My son said, "11-B," thinking she meant my shoe size. We all got a big laugh out of that one!*

Liz: Do you see any connection between your size and your sense of humor?

Jeanne: *Yes, but I credit my parents for that. They helped me see the humor in it at an early age, and taught me how to use humor to help others be as comfortable with my height as I was. There's a big difference between being self-deprecating — always bringing up the size issue yourself in a negative way — and having fun with your size when the situation calls for it.*

Liz: You often say, in print and in person, that you weigh 160 pounds. That's actually low for your height, isn't it? Yet do people seem surprised?

Jeanne: *Yes, it seems big to them, especially if they are 5'2" and weigh 120 pounds! One advantage of being taller is I can gain five pounds and no one notices except me.*

Liz: What encouragement would you offer a woman who is struggling with her size and self-esteem?

Jeanne: *Two suggestions. First of all, it's an acceptance thing. You have certain things you either have to change or accept about yourself, and size is one of those things. For example, I could probably change my southern accent, if I really wanted to and thought it was worth the effort. But I don't want to, so I accept it and learn to have fun with it. Second, I recommend using your sense of humor. Now remember, a sense of humor is not telling jokes. It's laughing at yourself and at life, seeing the humor in your circumstances. A person who has a sense of humor can usually handle anything. Fortunately, that is not a gift you receive at birth, it is a choice. A sense of humor is not inherited, it's developed. And I, for one, think it's worth developing, especially by us "larger-sized" folks.*

"You'll Never Get a Man"

A few years ago, I was hunched over my Delta Air Lines tray table, writing an article called, "What Makes Women Laugh?" The fella next to me studied the title at the top of my legal pad and chuckled. "That's easy!" he said. "Men!"

Well, since you brought it up, sir, sometimes we do find men laughable. Loveable, too. But sometimes we fear they won't love us back because we don't fit the size and shape of American beauty.

According to a 1988 Gallup Poll commissioned by *American Health* magazine, the average American man doesn't even think in terms of dress sizes when he's envisioning the kind of woman he would like to call his own. What he wants is a woman with an ample rear end, medium hips, a small-to-medium waist and medium-sized breasts. An average, not thin, body is his preference, and softer tone, not muscular.

Isn't it nice to know the "hard body" look is not particularly appealing to most men? For those of us whose size is well above average, do not despair! Remember, this is just the *average* response from men, which means others would have chosen bigger everything (and would therefore love us!).

Here's another fun note from my mailbox, written by a woman in Indiana. It seems this woman went on a cruise with three thin, tanned female friends. She was married (with a very trusting husband at home) and they were all single. Whom do you suppose got the flowers delivered to her room, got invited to exotic places and in general was the belle of the ball? Our plump note-writer, of course. She decided that Caribbean men like women who are "meaty!" Almost everywhere except the United States, women with more flesh are found to be more attractive.

I remember when I was trying to find a plus-size wedding gown and was getting desperate. At the eleventh hour, I considered finding a good seamstress to make one for me. I was referred to a sweet German woman who asked my dress size. "Twenty," I gulped.

"Oh, good, then you'll have a pretty neck and bosom!" she exclaimed. "We could do something nice and off the shoulder for you." Fascinating. To her foreign (literally) way of thinking, ample flesh was definitely an asset. Maybe we were all meant to be European!

Men and Size Preferences

If you looked only at polls like the one mentioned above, or glanced at the personals section of any newspaper where all the ads request thin women, it would be easy to surmise that ALL men want a small woman — or an average woman — but not a big woman. Oh, really? Then how do you explain all the men who are happily married to large women? A fluke? A mistake? Hardly. These men love their women who happen to be larger women.

> *My husband says nothing but positive stuff, which means a lot to me.*
>
> Mary Jane from Kentucky

These men may love their wives or girlfriends *because* of their size (and indeed, some men are "Fat Admirers," who simply are attracted to larger women).

> *My husband is a rare breed — he prefers large women. He thinks I'm still a little thin at 180 pounds.*
>
> Jill from Ohio

Or, a man may love his sweetie in spite of her size (perhaps she gained weight after marriage, and he has wisely chosen to accept it).

My #1 wonderful husband says he doesn't love me for my size — that I'm still precious and desirable.

Rosanne from Kentucky

Size is a non-issue with some men, and they would love us at any weight.

My husband says, "You're the prettiest girl in the world."

Sherry from Missouri

Hubby says, "More to love."

Bonita from Colorado

The Great Manhunt

Women who are single but long to be married often think they're doomed to remain unwed if they're not pencil thin. Most of them work at getting or staying lean for those hard-to-lasso hunks:

Since I am not married, I try to stay in shape to catch a man and because I want to.

Robin from Ohio

For the rest of us who may not be "in shape" but definitely are "shaped out," we sometimes conclude we're single *because* we're larger:

I don't have any relationships due to the fact that I'm fat. Always a friend, but never a girlfriend.

Lucia from Louisiana

I have not dated in several years. I assume this is because of my size although I'm not actively pursuing any men.

Debra from Washington

I certainly would have found myself agreeing with these women in 1985, when I hadn't dated in almost three years. I had finally "taken my name off the list," as it were. I was sick to death of being "fixed up" by my friends, as if I were somehow "broken," instead of just single.

Growing up, I always assumed I'd get married someday. It might have helped if I dated the right kind of men. Before becoming a Christian, all the men I dated were either married, separated, or happily single and avoiding commitment. Maybe they cared about my size, maybe they didn't. For certain, they didn't care enough for me to say, "I do."

After my conversion at age twenty-seven, you'll remember I dieted myself down to a slinky size 10. Men were still not beating a path to my door. So much for the, "If I lose weight, I'll get a man" theory. I stayed single and, for the most part, dateless until I met Bill in 1985, just before my thirty-first birthday.

What happened in those three man-free years? I gained weight! And, I gained self-confidence. They didn't come together as a package, but rather in sequence. When I put my weight back on, I lost all the false body confidence that comes from dieting. I had to develop, from ground zero, a whole new foundation of body confidence. This time, though, it was built on things that last and matter: God's love for me, and my love and respect for myself.

I never intentionally skipped marriage, it just happened that way. I woke up on my thirtieth birthday and said, "Oh my word, I forgot to get married!" The women in my church were always fussing over me, trying hard not to feel sorry for me, though they obviously did. "A-w-w-w-w," they'd say. "No husband? No children? Poor thing!" More than once, they intoned, "God has a man for you." (To which I always said, "Hey! He knows my address, what's the holdup?")

But, they were right. God did have a man for me. And He wisely waited until I was at peace with myself. He waited until I had a close relationship with Him, until I no longer needed a man in order to be happy. Then, Bill walked into my life. Great timing. I didn't overwhelm him with an eager, "Oh boy! A live one!" attitude.

I was initially introduced to Bill at a concert one warm June evening. I liked him immediately. He has an easy way about him — friendly, laid-back, warm. He was obviously bright, had a nice deep Kentucky twang and freckles all over. We met only briefly, but I thought, "What a nice man! I hope our paths cross again!"

They did. At a wedding. (No, not ours!) Just three weeks later, I dragged myself to a ceremony for two good friends. I say "dragged" because when you are single, weddings are lethal. We're talking big time bummer for days afterwards.

It just so happened the woman getting married was named "Liz," so the whole time she was taking her vows, I took them with her. (Just practice, you understand, in case I got to do it myself someday.) When the minister said, "Do you, Liz, take Doug?" I whispered under my breath, "I do!"

(After all, he was good looking – even if already spoken for by the other Liz!)

When the ceremony ended and I looked around the church to see who else I might know, there in the sea of pairs was a spare about two rows back: Bill! I studied his handsome, prematurely silver hair that was on full retreat from his forehead and thought, "I wonder how old he is? Thirty-five? Could be. Forty-five? Fifty-five? Whatever he is, he's just right!" I headed enthusiastically in his direction.

We talked until the church was empty. We talked at the reception until everyone else had gone home. I gave him my business card (with my home phone number on the back), and told him to "call me sometime."

"Sometime" came about five days later. Our first date was July 15, 1985. By October, we were in love. By Thanksgiving, engaged. At Christmas, I got my diamond ring (is this sounding too sappy?). We were married at 7:00 P.M., March 14, 1986. Three hundred people came to our wedding (probably to see if it would really happen!). It happened. Seven years later, it's still happening. I am more crazy about this man today than the day I married him.

A Better Class of Man

> *[Tell me] how to get a man to like you for your brain and humor, not for your looks.*
>
> Lori from Florida

Not all men are as wonderful as my Bill. Some are so short-sighted they can't see your intelligence and sense of humor. Too bad, because those things will last a lifetime. "Looks" as we define them grind to a halt somewhere between age sixteen and . . . well, too soon, anyway.

Carole Shaw of *BBW*, advises women: "If you want to meet a better class of man, put on twenty pounds!" Her point is well taken: the kind of man you want will not be so focused on body shape and size that he misses your wonderful mind and big, beautiful heart.

More than one woman can tell the sad tale of how she lost weight, hooked a man who loved her thin body, gained the weight back, and lost that shallow man.

> *Men are far more friendly when I'm at my low weights.*
>
> Michele from Indiana

> *My husband says, "Honey, you just sparkle when you lose a few pounds."*
>
> Jeddie from South Carolina

I grow weary of all these "what will a man think?" approaches to weight loss motivation. In an article titled, "The ABC'S of How to be Hungry and Like It," the author quotes Dr. Peter Miller of the Sea Pines Behavioral Institute at Hilton Head, South Carolina: "Imagine that your boyfriend is flirting with a slender, attractive girl instead of talking to you because you are eating an ice cream cone and your bulges are showing."

I say, stick the ice cream cone down his bathing suit and move on!

Don't Love Me (or Leave Me) Because of My Body

The fact is, men not only date, but also fall in love with and marry women who wear a size 16 or bigger. I admit when I looked at wedding pictures of my custom-built size 20 gown, I heaved a big sigh. No, I had never imagined myself as a big bride. But if Bill loved me "as is," I had married the right man, and *that* was something to celebrate!

> *My husband says he loves ME, not my dress size.*
>
> Diane from Tennessee

We are lucky, Diane. More than one husband does not affirm his wife or her body:

> *"You're so pretty — if only you would lose weight!" These are my husband's favorite words!*
>
> Barbara from Pennsylvania

Because large men are more tolerated in our society than large women, an unusual double standard can be employed:

> *My husband (who happens to have a big tummy) calls me "Fat Back" and is constantly telling me I need to diet.*
>
> Sally from Missouri

Other women wrote about husbands who called them, "Porky," "Fatty Fingers," "My Little Chubby One," "Big Boss," and "Miss Piggy."

> *My ex-husband always laughingly called me "Bubble Butt." He didn't seem to know or care that it hurt.*
>
> Sherry from Missouri

> *My ex-husband had several favorite nicknames he used to call me: Thunder Thighs, Tons of Fun, Mammoth Petite.*
>
> Vicky Lynn from Ohio

(One wonders if such nicknames were part of the reason these last two are "ex" husbands!)

The Double (Chin) Standard

Some husbands use our weight as their excuse to bail out:

> *[My size] was one of the reasons my ex-husband left, except I was only about 40 pounds overweight.*
>
> Janet from Kentucky

Good grief! If women left their husbands because *they* gained 40 pounds, the divorce rate would be at about 80%! People would think it shameful (and rightfully so, I might add), but society seems to accept the reverse. They'll put the blame on a woman, shake their heads and say, "Well, she shouldn't have let herself go."

> *If I lost 40 pounds, I'd have to spend all my time fighting men off with sticks.*
>
> Kathy from Michigan

What is this thing about "40 pounds?" Any man who would begin a relationship with you if you were 40 pounds thinner, but not today, is a dolt. Trust me, I dated plenty of them.

One young man in particular assured me that he would be happy to introduce me to his family and friends "just as soon as I lost 50 pounds." My self-esteem was so low at the time, I just shrugged and said, "I'll keep trying." Even now, as I write these words, I feel the pain of that moment and it makes me so angry I could spit.

If we allow men to hold such sway over our lives that we starve our bodies to attract them, and they subsequently desert us when we begin to eat again, then something is desperately wrong with both them *and* us.

We don't even like to eat around men. Think about your dating years. The guys got popcorn at the movie: we had two bites, they ate the rest. We stopped at McDonald's on the way home: they got a burger and fries, we got a diet drink. A single man in his early thirties once said that he knew a relationship with a woman was getting somewhere "when she was willing to eat more than a spinach salad in front of him."[1]

Thank Goodness for the Good Ones

Lest this appear as some strident attack against men, it's truly not. I like men. I have a father and three brothers. I married a man. And I gave birth to a male. Men are terrific (and quite necessary for the perpetuation of humankind!). Sometimes, they see us more accurately than we see ourselves:

My husband thinks I'm beautiful and I'm really not.
                                                    Connie from Pennsylvania

If he thinks you're beautiful, don't argue! Congratulate him on having the good sense to marry you.

It's time to hear from the Good Guys, the significant sweeties who are willing to love us "as is":

My husband says, "Your body is a testament of your life and I love it."
                                                    Carla from New Hampshire

My husband says don't worry about it. You look good to me.

Betty from Kentucky

My significant other thinks I'm beautiful.

Tami in Nebraska

My Bill always tells me (and sometimes with actions instead of words) that he finds me very attractive. If he did absolutely nothing else in his whole life, loving me when I sometimes resist it might be his most amazing accomplishment.

Those of us who grew up with (or grew into) a false belief that we couldn't possibly be appealing to a man are always amazed when one breaks through our self-imposed barriers and climbs into our hearts. When they love us, an amazing thing happens: we are set free to completely love ourselves and return their love as well.

Listen to Vicky Lynn's journey on this road:

When I discovered that I was going to have to face the world alone, I was heartsick thinking that no one in their right mind would want a "fat and forty" date. Then, at a Christian fellowship singles event, I realized my size was not that critical and what I had going for me was an infectious sense of humor. Strangers actually like me for who I am... and you know what? I LIKE ME!

Vicky Lynn from Ohio

Hooray for her! Whether or not she "gets her man," this woman has found joy, peace and fellowship. In the bargain, she's also discovered she has a lot to offer this world. Chances are, with a personality like that, she *will* have to "fight men off with a stick!"

Begin Building Body Confidence Today

1. Imagine yourself a writer of romance fiction and create a story in your mind of a big, beautiful, brilliant woman who is wildly pursued by a handsome, wise and witty man. They both weigh at least forty pounds over the insurance table desired weights and are having the time of their lives. Hollywood will never produce this story, so you will have to do it in your head. You decide . . . what's the happy ending?

2. Think of the men in your life who said, "I'd love you more IF..." or "IF you'd just lose some weight, I'd marry you..." or whatever conditional lines you may have heard. Forgive yourself for letting such messages pierce your heart. Forgive them for saying such unkind things. Not because they deserve it. Because you deserve to be set free from the pain that those comments still inflict when they bubble up unexpectedly.

3. Know that any man worth having in your life will find you desirable exactly as you are right now. If a man tells you that you're beautiful, believe him!

❤ A Husband Speaks . . .

My husband, William Robert Higgs (better known as Bill), has a Ph.D. in Hebrew from Southern Baptist Theological Seminary and is a computer systems specialist for a television station in Louisville. (You're right, those two areas do not compute. I call him my Renaissance Man!) Bill responded to the following questions on paper while I was presenting a program in Memphis. I asked him to be completely honest, in order to help us all better understand how men think.

Liz: What were your first thoughts when we were introduced on that June evening under the stars at Iroquois Amphitheater?

Bill: *It was only a fleeting meeting, but I was impressed immediately by your warmth and spirit, and by your confidence. You seemed very comfortable with who you were. I had dated a number of women who seemed to expect me to provide all their self-confidence for them. In your case, self-confidence was apparent from the outset.*

Liz: Did my size make any impression on you?

Bill: *Not in any particularly negative sense. What struck me was that your personality and confidence level did not match what I had come to associate with larger women. You didn't fit that image at all. Some men say they are turned off by larger women, and this may be so for a few. I would venture to say that their negative impression is mainly due to an attitude shown by some larger women rather than size itself. For me, at least, my attitude toward a woman is based mostly on her attitude toward herself.*

Liz: What made you decide to ask me out to dinner the following month?

Bill: *I liked you the minute we met and felt immediately comfortable around you. You were someone I needed to know better on a personal level, whether a long-term relationship grew out of it or not.*

Liz: Had you ever dated a larger woman before?

Bill: *Yes, although I had dated women of all shapes and sizes. Remember I was in my early thirties when we met, so my dating experience had been long and varied. For what it's worth, the last three women I dated before our meeting were all petite.*

Liz: After we became friends, did your view of my appearance change at all?

Bill: *Perhaps, but in a positive way. As I fell more and more in love with you, I became less and less aware of size. Other things had become much more important. In that sense, you had given me permission. Size had become a non-issue.*

Liz: Do you ever find yourself wishing I were thinner, or that I would go on a diet?

Bill: *Not often, and only if I sense your self-confidence is sagging or if you have indicated that you want to lose weight. There is a fine line between supporting someone in their desire to lose weight and making them feel as though they are unaccepted otherwise. I have walked that line a few times during our marriage, as you have struggled with whether to diet or not. If losing weight were truly your desire, I would support you in it. BUT, if I felt you were doing so because you no longer felt you met my expectations, I would probably discourage you from dieting.*

Liz: Are you ever embarrassed to introduce me to someone as your wife?

Bill: *Never. I am very proud of you.*

Liz: You have gained a few pounds since we married (though not as much as I have!). Has your size had any effect on how you feel about yourself? Any effect on our relationship?

Bill: *I don't feel it has affected either in any particular way. I wouldn't mind losing a few pounds, but I don't think my self-esteem has suffered any from my weight gain. For men, the pressures are not so much from the standpoint of appearance, but rather physical prowess or ability. I have never been much of an athlete, nor have I had any particular obsession with looking slim and trim. If losing weight would give me a bit more stamina or ward off future health problems, I might give it more thought. My guess is that turning forty has probably had more effect on my energy level than gaining weight. I am one of those men who spent most of their youth trying to gain weight rather than lose it — I did not reach my "textbook" weight until I was nearly thirty. As far as our relationship is concerned, I haven't noticed any particular effect. It just makes it easier to let you throw out my old pants that don't fit anymore!*

Liz: What would you say to a man who says, "No woman of mine will ever be fat!"

Bill: *To a married man I would say, "You may not have that choice, because your wife may not have that choice." To a single man I would say, "You've severely limited your options." Unfortunately, this kind of attitude is typical of a certain male viewpoint which still sees a wife or girlfriend as a possession, or worse, a status symbol. Possessions and symbols, by their very nature, are transient and can be discarded at will. The problem is a basic misunderstanding of what a relationship is supposed to be. Such a man can expect problems in a relationship with any woman, large or small. I wonder what he might say to a woman who declared, "No man of mine will ever be bald!" Physical attributes change over time for both men and women. Maybe he should forget women and buy a dog instead. He'd be happier!*

Liz: How would you encourage a man to love his wife, no matter what her size?

Bill: *Never make love conditional on her physical appearance (or anything else, for that matter).*

Liz: How would you encourage a woman to please her beloved, no matter what her size?

Bill: *Always assume that you are attractive to him, whether you feel attractive or not. If he says you are beautiful, he's right. If a woman's husband rejects her appearance, this would certainly be tougher for her. I would still say, however, that the key is believing you are desirable. You alone are master of your image and personality. Don't let anyone else (Hollywood, husbands or fashion) define them for you.*

"You Can Lose It If You Really Want To"

One spring, I presented a luncheon program for a small group of executive wives while their husbands conducted business down the hall. They were a fun bunch, beautifully dressed, well-educated, witty and warm. But all they talked about at lunch was how FAT they were. Not one woman in the room could have weighed more than five to ten pounds over the standard weight chart statistics for her height and age, but to them that was positively obese.

The woman sitting directly across from me waited for the right moment to announce that she had just lost 80 pounds.

"Imagine," she said, "I used to wear a size 22 jacket and a size 24 skirt!" Everyone gasped, then praised her for her dieting success.

There I sat, their invited guest speaker, wearing a size 22 jacket and a size 24 skirt. I didn't know whether to laugh or cry. Maybe, I thought, I should ask her if she has any old clothes she'd like to share with me! Before long, she was looking me straight in the eye and saying, "Anyone can lose 80 pounds if they want to badly enough."

"I'm not sure that's true," I said softly. "I believe metabolically and genetically, it would be almost impossible for me to lose and keep off 80 pounds."

She shook her head and rolled her eyes in disgust. "You just haven't really tried," she insisted. It was obvious I wasn't about to change her mind, so I simply smiled and let it drop, praying that the women around us would soon find another topic of conversation.

They didn't.

"Say What?"

What do you say when people suggest, boldly or in a roundabout way, that you could or should lose weight? Society seems to delight in presenting this option to us at every turn, as if we haven't already thought it through and tried dozens of diets. Dr. Albert Stunkard, an obesity researcher at the University of Pennsylvania, found that, "There's that implicit assumption that you really could lose weight if you settled down and stopped being such a fat slob."[1] Dr. Stunkard knows better, and so do we.

Judith from Colorado echoed that false conclusion people often make. "'If large women don't like it, they would lose it.' Get real." The societal assumption is that: 1) We don't know we are fat, so they have to point it out to us. 2) We haven't *really* tried to lose weight.

My first exposure to self-acceptance came almost a decade ago when I tried to start a diet group at work. One woman I was certain would want to sign up immediately said, "No thanks!" I was shocked. She was the first larger woman I'd ever met who was comfortable with her self. She didn't live each day apologizing for her size or vowing to start back on a diet next Monday. She's the same size today she was ten years ago. I think she's on to something!

Most of the time, when people suggest the "D" word to me, I smile and say, "I've decided that diets don't work, and so instead I'm learning to accept myself at this size."

They usually respond with something like, "That's great!" and quickly change the subject. If they come back with, "But what about your health?" I share some of the statistics included in this book.

As Carole Shaw pointed out: "Look in a hospital. Do you think in every one of those rooms is a fat person?" Sometimes a simple statement like that can get a person's mental wheels turning. Another favorite quotable quote from Carole, also from her appearance on the

Jenny Jones show: "In a hundred years, all of us are gonna weigh the same!"[2]

Give people time to accept where you are. Look how long it's taken some of us to wake up to the truth about dieting, weight-loss scams and health risks (or the lack of them). We have a long way to go before we convince the average American woman that we know what we're talking about. Patience will be required to make it through this educational process.

The Last Straw

There are times when I run out of the virtue of patience. An example comes to mind: It was the first day I met with my talented, red-headed editor from Thomas Nelson — the man who believed my message and in my ability to put it into words.

Duncan and I were enjoying lunch in a busy open-air restaurant in La Jolla, California, on a lovely Sunday afternoon in August. The sun was shining, the breeze was blowing, and we were having a wonderful time tossing ideas back and forth about this book-in-progress.

A woman seated at the table next to us kept eyeing me and smiling in my direction. Finally, she came over and introduced herself. "My name is Barb, and I couldn't help overhearing your conversation." (That's probably true, because neither Duncan nor I talk softly!)

She continued, "I thought you might like to know about a product I sell that offers an all-natural approach to weight control."

I have never done this before or since, but I did it that day. "Ma'am, YOU might like to know that I am highly offended that you would be so bold as to suggest that I need, or want, to lose weight!"

She started doing a very quick social two-step. "Oh, I didn't mean to suggest that you need to lose weight, I . . . uh, just thought with the book you were discussing, you needed to know about this."

Right. It was very obvious what she was suggesting. People are so certain fat people want to be thin people, they think nothing of accosting complete strangers and offering their sure-fire "solutions."

Admittedly, I embarrassed her terribly. (My editor ended up apologizing on my behalf!) But sometimes, enough is enough.

Laura Eljaiek, now Program Director of the National Association to Advance Fat Acceptance, tells the story of having a man behind her on the bus suggest, "You could use some Slim Fast." Her quick comeback? "You could use some manners!"[3]

File It Under "They Meant Well"

When strangers say rude things, we can ignore it, nail them with a caustic reply, or laugh. In any case, soon they are out of our lives, and the sting of their words is quickly dulled.

But when friends comment on our size or weight, the knife is sharper, cuts deeper, and leaves a more gaping wound. In almost every situation, friends are trying to say the right thing, and instead step on their own tongue (and our toes):

> *My pseudo friends say, "Isn't it a shame you're so large — you're so attractive!"*
>
> Diana from Kentucky

> *Women say, "You don't act like a big person." (Figure that out!)*
>
> Melissa from Ohio

They may watch us for diet signals, so they can be sure to offer just the right word of encouragement:

> *If I'm hungry and I don't eat, my coworkers ask, "Are you on a DIET? Are you trying to lose WEIGHT?"*
>
> Dolores from New York

If you need a reason to tell people why you have given up on dieting, here's one of the best ones: Diets are a no-win, no-lose proposition. In a recent newspaper survey of local weight loss centers, one center admitted that 75% of their clients had to return to their program. "After two or three years, almost everybody comes back."[4]

What kind of success record is that? And what damage has been done to clients' self-esteem and metabolism in the meantime? At least that particular program was being honest. Of the seven interviewed, four stated that the data on returnees was "not available."[5] Uh-huh.

Even weight control programs that include behavior modification and a full year of maintenance don't fare well. In one study, women participated in a sixteen-week weight loss program, followed by a twelve-month maintenance program. At the start, their average weight was 214. Thirty months after the program, their average weight was 217.[6] Something is wrong here, and it's not the women.

A recent issue of the newsletter *Obesity and Health* took a strong stance against many of the methods of weight loss being offered in today's marketplace. "Exploitation, deception, greed and fraud are common. Many treatments are health-threatening, causing injury and even death."[7]

Some women have a deceptively simple way to "diet": they smoke cigarettes. About 10% of women who start smoking do so to lose weight. Some 25% of women who now smoke use cigarettes to control their weight and are therefore afraid to quit.[8] Because smoking makes the heart work harder, it does raise your metabolic rate a bit. But more than 400, 000 Americans died from cigarette smoking in 1991 alone.[9] As diets go, smoking is a killer.

This may be the hardest thing I'll ever say, but by putting it in print, I'll be duty-bound to honor it. I'm never going to diet again. Period. As author Rita Freedman says, "Dieting entails narcissistic self-preoccupation and masochistic self-denial."[10] Neither one of those sound like the path to righteousness that "shines ever brighter unto the perfect day."[11] In fact, it sounds downright gloomy!

When someone starts singing their, "But, what about your health?" tune, why not offer some statistical proof that *dieting* can be hazardous to your health, often more so than carrying extra weight.

Specifically, Freedman warns that "the chronic dieter may suffer from malnutrition, gastric problems, irritability, anxiety, lethargy, fatigue, tension, insomnia and depression."[12] The more drastic the diet, the more dangerous. For example, 25% of people on very low calorie diets (like the liquid kind) develop gallstones.[13] No fun.

Those of us who gain, lose, gain, lose are taking the most risks of all. Research shows that people with high weight variability (us "yo-yo's") are 25-100% more likely to experience heart disease and premature death than people whose weight remains stable.[14] Even those who are data-resistant and refuse to let a little thing like research get in the way of an old belief system would have to pause at that chilling statistic on the dangers of weight cycling.

Guess Who's *Not* Coming to Dinner

What do you say when someone tells you they are on a diet? I don't want to encourage them, but naturally I don't want to *dis*courage them, either. My solution is to say, "I will love and respect you whether you lose, gain or stay the same. Just for the record, you're an attractive and wonderful person right now!"

I also fight the urge to talk someone into eating something they don't want to eat. After all, whether I agree with them or not, they have the right to choose what foods they put in their body. The whole subject of eating and dieting is a very personal one. I do, however, stand ready to support a friend when, as so often happens, the diet doesn't work. At that time of discouragement, a kind word, assurance that they have lots of company (95% of dieters) and a reminder it's not their "fault" can be welcome words. The key is to offer unconditional love.

I recently picked up a brochure on the latest fasting-based diet (I read such things for amusement) and couldn't help noticing that these women looked better in their "before" pictures than they did in their "after" photos! They looked so gaunt and frail after their "doctor-supervised" fasts that you wanted to sit them down to a decent meal and help them regain their strength.

David the psalmist saw the same phenomenon: "My knees are weak through fasting,/And my flesh is feeble from lack of fatness."[15]

There's No Denying It

There's more than one form of denial.

Some women deny that they are fat. They run past mirrors, dress in the dark, wear very loose clothing and just pretend it's not there. They cut out the labels in their clothing, stick to sizes that end in X, and list their dress size as 14-16, when the truth is they haven't worn a size 14 for many years. They do *not* read *BBW* magazine, they read *Ladies Home Journal* or *Redbook*.

Another kind of denial: Some women would call themselves "overweight," but temporarily so. They think they can diet it off anytime, like the smoker who says she can quit anytime, but never gets around to it. These women subscribe to *Weight Watchers* magazine, and go on a diet the first Monday of almost every month. They've joined weight groups half a dozen times, but never made it to the diamond pin. They see their weight as a sign of laziness or lack of willpower. As soon as they have more time, they'll get the weight off.

A third kind of denial: These women are former fat women who have dieted themselves down to an almost-acceptable weight. I say "almost" because I've never met a woman who actually weighed her goal weight. They always say to another woman, "Just seven more pounds to go!" These women are often very self-righteous. They unwittingly look down their noses at every woman who weighs ten pounds more than they do. "I'll never be like that again," they think to themselves. They read *Self* and *Glamour*, and walk past the mirror often. (It's really not their fault they have this attitude, it's just the lack of nutrition. Like Sherry from Michigan says, "Stay out of my way when I'm dieting! I'm grouchy!")

Where did my definitions of these three forms of denial come from? The research project called My Life. Please don't hear judgment in my words, just the truth as I see it.

Here are my findings: being fat does not necessarily mean a person is living in denial; being thin is definitely no guarantee against living in denial. The reality is that all of us are in a state of denial about something. There's no denying this, though: God loves us in whatever state we are in (geographical or spiritual).

The View from the Other Side

Of the more than 200 surveys compiled for this book, only one was from a woman who had recently lost quite a bit of weight. Because she is a dear friend of mine, she was willing to complete the survey anyway. I love her too much to include her name here, but I want to share her words. When I lost 45 pounds back in 1984, this is almost exactly what I might have written myself:

> *The difference between weighing 205 and 135 is so great it can't be explained. Everyone — from store clerks you don't even know to your own husband — treats you differently, more respectfully, when you're thin. And because we are products of the same society we are part of, we treat ourselves differently when we can smile at the reflection in the mirror.*

What is wrong with this picture? Store clerks should treat you with respect no matter what you weigh (whatever happened to "the customer is always right?"). Of all people, your husband should respect you, thick or thin. The Bible commands it: "Husbands, love your wives." Period. No parenthetical, "but if she weighs 205 pounds, treat her like dirt." No way.

Most importantly, we need to smile at the reflection in the mirror *no matter what the size of the woman smiling back*! Because here is the awful truth, and the reason dieting is so dangerous to our emotional well-being: If we gain back some or all of the weight we lost (and remember the odds of that happening are 19 in 20), then how will we feel about that woman in the mirror? What kind of treatment will we think we deserve from our husbands and loved ones? What kind of grief will we put up with from store clerks who are rude to us?

Society will *not* change how it views or treats us until *we* change how we view ourselves and how we treat one another. Susan Wooley, Ph.D., the woman who did the *Glamour* survey in 1984, said, "If shame could cure obesity, there wouldn't be a fat woman in the world."[16]

Look Who's On Our Side

Support for body acceptance, for letting go of perfect, is beginning to come from all corners of our world, both statistical support as well as emotional. Even the medical community is coming around, although slowly. I love the note I received from an Ohio woman who told me about her mother's trip to the hospital at age forty-five. Her tall, skinny doctor ordered his large, lovely patient to go on a 600 calorie a day diet, and instructed the nurse to keep a close eye on her. One week later, without cheating one iota, the woman had gained two pounds. Now, twenty-seven years later, she still has the same doctor, and he has never mentioned her weight again. Bravo!

Here's some authoritative support from an unexpected place. The Smithsonian Museum in Washington, D.C., had an exhibit on display a few years ago titled "Clothes, Gender and Power." It included a whole display cabinet full of diet books, diet products, diet pills and fitness videos. Near the cabinet was displayed this poster:

FAT

- There is no known cause of obesity.
- There is no known cure.
- Obese people do not on the average eat more than anyone else.
- Ninety percent of Americans who lose weight through dieting gain it back within two years.
- There is little scientific evidence to prove that obesity causes high blood pressure or heart disease.

- Slightly overweight people live longer than thin people.
- Taking amphetamines, fasting, undergoing gastric stapling or constantly gaining and losing weight are dangerous to your health.[17]

Thank you, United States Government!

Begin Building Body Confidence Today

1. Decide exactly how you want to respond to people who suggest that you should lose weight. If you plan what you want to say in advance, you are less likely to hurt their feelings or have your own damaged. Something gentle, loving, firm, even informational might work for you.

2. Choose the right way to respond to someone who tells you that *they* want to lose weight. Don't encourage dieting, but do affirm their decision. Again, sensitivity is the key, and perhaps offering some information (or a copy of this book!).

3. Find your own support network, *not* a diet group, to help you grow in the right direction. A circle of friends, a walking group, a Bible study, a weekly lunch gathering, whatever works for you. What matters is that you love and encourage each other without any conditions or judgments.

❤ A Support Group Leader Speaks . . .

Carol Johnson is the Founder and President of Largely Positive, Inc., in Milwaukee, Wisconsin. She earned her master's degree in applied sociology from Kent State University in Ohio. She is a certified psychotherapist, and is currently doing research in mental health.

Liz: Tell us about your journey toward becoming Largely Positive.

Carol: *I am a lifelong larger woman. About five years ago, I was browsing through a bookstore for a new diet book to try and stumbled on* The Dieter's Dilemma: Eating Less and Weighing More *by William Bennett, M.D., and Joel Gurin. The title really intrigued me, because I sure was in a dilemma! I thought it would finally tell me what was wrong with me, why I couldn't lose weight. When I finished reading the book, I just wanted to find the authors and kiss them! It seemed my weight struggles were not my fault after all.*

Liz: What happened next?

Carol: *I started reading all the research on obesity (ugh, I hate that word, but that's what they call it in the medical community), and I began discovering many research findings that no one had ever told me about. It really made me angry, especially at my doctors, because the information wasn't even brand new, it had been around a while. I've since discovered that what most people believe about obesity and what the research really says are two entirely different things.*

Liz: [Laughing] It's been an educational process for most of us, rethinking the whole diet thing. Where did the Largely Positive idea come from?

Carol: *I remember the night it was born. I had been going with a friend to Diet Workshop (you know, one I hadn't tried yet), and I was losing my usual quarter to half pound a week. The woman weighing me kept giving me these "you're not really trying" looks, but I had read all the research and knew that losing slowly was much healthier than losing five pounds a week of water. Anyway, the 4th of July was coming up, so that night she decided as a group exercise, "Let's make a list of all the freedoms we lose when we are overweight." Something snapped. I raised my hand and asked, "Why are we doing such a negative thing? Why are we doing this to ourselves?" I went home that night and said, "That's it! No more negative stuff. I want to go to a place that makes me feel positive about myself!"*

Liz: Who encouraged you to start your own support group?

Carol: *I owe a debt of gratitude to two Milwaukee area doctors. Drew Palin, M.D., president of Competitive Edge Sports Medicine, was also my husband's doctor. Fearful that Dr. Palin might tell my husband that his problems were all due to his weight, I armed my husband with Largely Positive literature and said, "If he says anything about your weight, give him this!" Imagine my amazement when my husband called me later that day and said, "Dr. Palin would like to meet you. He thinks your stuff is great." He's been collaborating with me ever since. One interesting note: Dr. Palin used to work with the Optifast program, but quit when he realized that all his patients were regaining their weight.*

Liz: What about the second doctor who helped you?

Carol: *That's Dr. Anthony Machi, a highly respected physician who treats patients with eating disorders. He was in the audience at one of my programs and afterwards approached me and said, "Is there anything I can do to help you?" Of course, I said, "Yes! I want to start a support group and we need somewhere to have our meetings." He convinced the hospital to provide not only space, but also marketing support and reimbursement for professional facilitators. We meet weekly at Milwaukee Psychiatric Hospital. In addition to Dr. Machi, the hospital has a wonderful team of therapists, all of whom* support and promote our group to their patients. I consider Shay Harris, M.S.W., a larger woman herself, as my partner in Largely Positive.*

Liz: How many people have come through your door?

Carol: *I have five hundred names on our mailing list, and about 125 people who subscribe to our quarterly newsletter, On a Positive Note. An average meeting for our weekly discussion night might include twenty to twenty-five people. Our monthly meetings with a guest speaker will draw forty to fifty people.*

Liz: What kinds of issues do you address in your support group?

Carol: *We primarily talk about self-esteem and living a healthy lifestyle. The issues of social prejudice, as well as problems with how large people are depicted in the media, also come up in our discussion groups. We don't talk about dieting, but we had an enlightened dietitian come in and talk about nutrition, as well as an exercise physiologist who spoke about how to exercise without getting hurt. Our emphasis is on wholeness and health. If, in the process of eating healthy foods and beginning to exercise, we become somewhat thinner, okay. If not, that's okay too. Weight loss is not our goal. Being positive about ourselves, and disassociating our self-esteem from our weight is our goal.*

Liz: How has your own body confidence developed?

Carol: *I no longer wear coats in the summertime! I now go to a pool three nights a week, and I'm no longer self-conscious about wearing a bathing suit.*

Liz: That is a big step!

Carol: *It breaks my heart when I see women weigh themselves before and after they exercise, as if that is the only way they can measure the value of swimming.*

Liz: Do you still weigh yourself?

Carol: *No, I threw my scale away years ago. I have a pretty good idea what I weigh and actually have lost some weight since starting Largely Positive. I never worry about numbers. We know from research that heredity plays a big part, and I had two wonderful, fat grandmothers, one who lived to eighty-five, one to ninety.*

Liz: How's your own level of self-esteem now?

Carol: *Before, I was trying to hide my bigness. Now I celebrate it! I wear big, bold jewelry, bright colors, and am not afraid to be expressive and dramatic.*

Liz: What is the heart of your message to larger women?

Carol: *Get out there and live your life. Don't postpone it until you get thin. That day may never come and you will have missed out on some wonderful adventures. Don't let anyone tell you you're not a worthwhile person just as you are. Like other groups who have been treated unfairly, we must demand to be treated with respect, dignity and understanding.*

"One Size Fits All"

Here's the biggest fable of all: that one size *anything* would fit a woman who is 5'1", 105 pounds *and* fit a woman who is 5'11", 270 pounds. To even suggest it is ridiculous. Oh, maybe a handkerchief would work for both of them, but not much else! As one survey respondent stated,

> *We are all individuals and "one size fits us all" very differently.*
> Judy from Ohio

Some manufacturers are wising up, and their labels now read, "One Size Fits Most." That still does nothing for my self-esteem, since I'm not one of the "most."

I received a Christmas catalogue last year featuring a pair of holiday pantyhose with jingle bells and holly stitched up and down each leg. (So professional-looking, this item.) The catalogue stated: "One Size Fits All (We Know, Because We All Tried Them On)."

Really? That's not very comforting to me. First of all, I've never visited that company and don't know if they have a woman on staff who is my exact size or not. And second of all, who wants used pantyhose?!

Another item that debuted last Christmas did ring my bell: the "Happy to Be Me" doll. Cathy Meredig of High Self-Esteem Toys Corporation wanted a doll for young girls that would look like a real person. Hooray for Cathy! If you gave the typical fashion doll a 36 inch bust, her measurements as a full-grown woman would be 36"-18"-33". Not too realistic, I'd say, and a terrible role model for our daughters.

The "Happy to Be Me" doll has a thicker waist and bigger feet than Barbie, and a shorter neck and legs. Plus, her feet fit sensible shoes (not just tippy-toe heels), and her arms bend in a more natural way. Will it help us teach the next generation to love their bodies "as is?" It couldn't hurt!

Someone might also consider revamping store window mannequins, whose average measurements are 33"-23"-34". Talk about one size that fits almost no one! Erma Bombeck says, "'One size fits all' is not listed in my dictionary under 'O.' This is because the phrase exists only in the maniacal minds of manufacturers."[1]

The Good Old Days

Maybe we were just born during the wrong period of history. In the 1600's, one diet specialist wrote that "Every thin woman wishes to put on weight."[2] Can you imagine? The paintings of the era, and the years that followed, cast an adoring eye on round, soft, full-of-flesh women. The works of Rubens in the early 1600's and Renoir in the early 1900's are famous for their display of feminine flesh. The first time I saw one of their paintings, I gasped out loud: "That's me!"

Ann Landers said it best: "What we need is a high-powered campaign to glorify the Rubenesque woman and get off the 'thin is in' kick."[3] You can imagine the letters of support she received on that one.

Although dieting and fitness fanaticism as we know it is a post-WWI phenomenon, women have been agonizing over society's expectations for their bodies for a long time. One woman bemoaned the narrowing of the American ideal saying, "When we see a woman made as a woman ought to be made, she strikes us as a monster."[4] Gloria Steinem? No, Harriet Beecher Stowe, circa 1830.

The time has come for the pendulum to swing back toward reality. I heartily applaud fitness expert Pat Lyons for announcing, "It is time to stop the merry-go-round of self-hatred, dieting and despair and work together to create a more size-accepting world for us all."[5]

Actually, one size has *never* fit all, because our bodies are shaped so differently. Since the 1930's, one of the most widely used means of body typing is called, "somatotyping," designed by William Sheldon. According to his methodology, there are some 2,197 possible body types.[6] (More than just pears and apples, it would seem.) These are genetically-determined body types, not just adult bodies with too many, or not enough, burgers and fries. Size acceptance should be everyone's goal since we all have a size that's uniquely our own.

Mind Over Matter

I've always wondered, who exactly we were trying to be thin for? Our parents? Our husbands? Our friends? Our employers? Ourselves? Society as a whole? Who held such sway over our bodies that we saw fit to starve ourselves into acceptance? I think the whole issue is one of mind over matter — if you don't mind, it won't matter!

Many of the two hundred plus women we surveyed have come to that same conclusion:

> *Now that I'm almost forty, I have become very happy and comfortable with my size. My kids are too. They love to tell me that I look just like Jane Fonda to them.*
>
> Jerri from Indiana

It's apparent that her good feelings about herself have extended to her family. In years to come, those children will have a positive role model to emulate when deciding how they feel about their own bodies.

> *The wonder and joy of life that is experienced by larger women is the same for all — one size does truly fit all in the whole scheme of things.*
>
> LaDonna from Oregon

We just need to look at the big picture. Joy certainly fits us all, love is plenty big enough for everybody, and peace could cover the earth, if we let it. In the meantime, we can work on bringing those qualities into our own lives and the lives of those we care about.

Putting What We Believe into Motion

Since I've become more self-assured, I rarely encounter people who judge me for my size.

Joyce from Virginia

Isn't it amazing how, if we feel okay about who we are, so does everyone else? Gwen from Ohio says, "I have learned to like who I am (no, love who I am). I feel good about me!"

Our call to action is beautifully stated by Sherry from Missouri, who said:

"Until Big, Beautiful Women change how they see themselves, there's no way the world will change how they see us. We need to stand up and be heard."

She's so right! I had to change how I saw myself before I could write this book. You had to be willing to change how you saw yourself to read it. Now, it's time to "stand up and be heard!" In America, we no longer openly tolerate racism (though of course it still rears its ugly head), and we have been fighting sexism more or less successfully for the last twenty-five years or so. Now, ageism is being defeated, as more and more baby boomers hit middle age and realize they want fair and equal treatment through retirement and beyond.

It's time to face, head on, the most insidious "ism" of all. Fatism. It's everywhere—on radio and television, in magazines and in newspapers, in the workplace and the classroom. Comedians still have a field day with fat jokes, doctors still hand out diets and dire predictions, parents still send their kids off to fitness camps, praying that they won't end up (heaven forbid) as fat people.

Fatism needs to be seen as the prejudicial problem that it really is. Author Charles Roy Schroeder notes that it would be helpful "if the term 'fatism' was listed in dictionaries along with the equally sinful traits of racism, sexism and ageism."[7] Amen.

One Size Fits No One

As we learned from the interview with tall humorist Jeanne Robertson, some of the challenges larger women face are not limited to those of us with additional poundage. "Big" doesn't just refer to weight. Tall women have their own struggles that closely match ours.

(Being) an Extra Large doesn't necessarily mean that you are big. Height takes up a lot of room in a shirt too!
                                                          Harriet from Louisiana

And, small women don't live on Easy Street, either!

People say things like, "How tall are you anyway?" or "What size shoe do you wear?" Children ask me, "When will you be full grown?"
                                                          Rose from South Carolina

My coworkers tell me I'm small, petite, cute — and disgusting.
                                                          Jeanie from Ohio

Mark Twain said, "I can live for two months on a good compliment." Maybe if we started offering kinder comments to one another, we could live longer. I know we'd all live happier.

Real winners (that's us!) know that success is not measured in inches and pounds. The first producer for the late Helen Hayes told her when she arrived in Hollywood, that "if you were just four inches taller, you would be a great actress." So much for that advice.

Several years ago, when Lillian was a newborn, I presented my program of this same title, "'One Size Fits All' and Other Fables," to a wonderful audience of eight hundred women of all ages, sizes, shapes and colors. When I finished, the woman who introduced me pulled a poem out of her briefcase. She thought it "suited perfectly" my message of self-acceptance. "You'll want to share it with your daughter when she's older," she said.

Since then, I've shared that verse from a poem by Douglas Malloch with thousands of women across America, as well as with Miss Lillian:

> If you can't be a highway, then just be a trail,
> If you can't be the sun, be a star.
> It isn't by size that you win or you fail,
> Be the best of whatever you are!

We're Not Alone

Among the many challenges that plus-sized women face — tight theater seats, hard-to-find fashions, and pantyhose disasters — the biggest one of all is a feeling of aloneness or isolation. It's not that we're hiding in our houses, it's just that we seldom have a place to go where we feel safe talking about some of these issues. At least one of the times I joined Weight Watchers, it was because I wanted to be in a roomful of women who weren't all thin! Unfortunately, since they were all trying to *get* thin, I didn't find the camaraderie I was hoping for.

According to your surveys, you, too, wanted to find fellowship among these pages:

> *Help me know I'm not alone in this never-ending battle to be slim, trim and gorgeous. Since I was born a Chubette and went straight to Full Blown it's not been easy.*
>
> Cory from North Carolina

No, it's not easy! We can say that here and know that those reading will understand. (For my money, I'd rather be full-figured than half-figured, any day!)

> *As with other women's issues, the consciousness-raising aspect is important — knowing we are not alone and that the barrier of shame is a greater handicap than a person's weight.*
>
> Fran from Illinois

"The barrier of shame" is a very accurate description of what many of us feel. Take note: guilt and shame are non-productive states. Guilt leads to hopelessness, defeat, and despair. Shame leads to isolation, separation, and a feeling of worthlessness. Enough of that. Enough for a lifetime, I'm certain.

A Benediction

> *This book will let all of us who read it know that our struggle is the same all over. And that we can make it through the hard times by laughing at things, rather than crying. If this had been around thirty*

*years ago I would have not wasted my teen years hiding out from
the big bad world — wearing a black coat.*

Lynda from California

I wish I could have written it for you thirty years ago, Lynda. That
was right about the time I first began thinking about dieting. May the
young women who follow in our footsteps be spared our pain (or at
least *this* pain!).

By the way, I still wear a black coat, but it's a zippy one. I also
have a red one, a purple one and a camel one, and they only get worn
when it's cold or wet! No more hiding.

As I come to the conclusion of this labor of love, a project that
kept me up late, got me up early, stole precious hours from my family,
brought tears to my eyes and joy to my soul, I wanted to tie it all
together with a ribbon of prayer.

Dear God,

I want to be healthy, happy and whole.
*I want to be all Yours, all Bill's, all my children's, all my audience's
and ALL MINE.*

Not all things to all people, Lord.
Just all there.

Bless those who have kindly read these pages.
*I pray these words have given them encouragement, hope and a
lighter heart.*

*Lord, may Your beauty and love shine through us all, and give us
confidence of mind, body and spirit — at any size!*

Amen

♥ A Size Acceptance Leader Speaks . . .

RADIANCE: The Magazine for Large Women has been published quarterly since 1984. Its creator, founder, editor, publisher and soul is Alice Ansfield of Oakland, California.

Liz: How did *RADIANCE* begin?

Alice: *It began a week after I found myself in an exercise class for plus-size women in 1984. I had been searching for a place to move my body in a setting where I felt safe and supported. Once I found it, I decided I wanted to do a little newsletter for the women in my exercise class. It was apparent that the class members weren't sure where to shop, how to find larger exercise clothes, and needed help feeling better about themselves. So,* RADIANCE *was born.*

Liz: Except it didn't remain a "little newsletter" for very long.

Alice: *That's right! Within two months, I had a twenty-page publication with twenty-eight advertisements! My initial intent was to distribute it just in the Oakland area, but as I began assembling names and addresses, I thought, "Why not keep going? Why not send copies all over the country?"*

Liz: How many copies of that first issue did you print?

Alice: *We printed five thousand copies in October 1984. People understood our concept right away, and the* San Francisco Chronicle *covered it. Soon, subscriptions started pouring in. We now have six thousand paid subscribers from all over the world.*

Liz: And, it's a bigger magazine too.

Alice: *Yes. Fifty-two glossy, radiant pages!*

Liz: I'm sure readers' responses are very important to you.

Alice: *They keep me going. When a new subscriber sends in an order, I'm the one who types their information into the*

computer. It keeps me connected to my readers. The very
first letter I received was from a fifty-five-year-old woman
in Maine who wrote, "Hurry up and send RADIANCE!
I've been hiding in my house for six years." I love to see
what people write on their gift cards. They are always such
loving, supportive comments like "I want the best for you,"
that kind of thing.

Liz: Have you received any criticism over the years?

Alice: *[Laughing] Of course! Especially early on. The first time
I put a supersize woman on the cover — a very successful
San Francisco attorney — I got a lot of flack from the
fashion community in L.A.: "Large women want to see the
fantasy of what they can look like, not the reality of what
they do look like," they said. Over the years, we've heard
that we have too much fashion, others say not enough. Or,
that we're too political, or not political enough. I do listen
to such feedback, but I have to stick with what feels right
to me. I must be true to myself, to my aims and my goals.*

Liz: What are some of the problems larger women face?

Alice: *A sense of shame. Self-hatred. Lack of support, lack of
trust in ourselves and our bodies. Rejection. Fear of
putting ourselves out there. There are some practical
challenges, too, like not being able to fit in restaurant
booths, theatre seats, airplane seats. Once, I was trying to
get into a health club and had trouble fitting through the
turnstile! We have a lot of work to do in our society!*

Liz: Are there any advantages to being a large woman?

Alice: *To me, being a large woman is just who I am. It's a part
of me. I also have a large heart and a large capacity for
fun. My experiences with my body have brought me more
in touch with myself, my feelings, needs, visions, and
abilities. My body has brought me opportunities to be
creative, learn about others and contribute to people's
lives. There are advantages to embracing all parts of
yourself — whatever situation you're in. And I might add
that it's getting easier to be a large person today — with all*

the support groups, clothing manufacturers and various services just for us!

Liz: What do you say when people comment, "Well, what about your health?"

Alice: *In my eight years of doing* RADIANCE, *I have heard more often than I can tell you the line, "dieting has made me fatter." I don't think you can achieve a state of positive health while hating your body. Emotional health and social well-being are two factors directly related to physical health. Ending discrimination of all kinds will do more for the health of large people than any new diet plan or well-meaning doctor. People need to find out what helps them feel good — what foods they enjoy, what types of movement their bodies are yearning for, what friends, jobs and activities bring pleasure. Health, obviously, is much more than how much you weigh or what size your waist is.*

Liz: What is the first step to accepting ourselves, "as is?"

Alice: *Self-acceptance is not an easy process. It's difficult to turn around our insecurities, attitudes and fears. Just take it one step at a time. Read one book, attend one lecture, find and talk to one other woman dealing with similar body issues. Try one thing and follow your heart.*

A Perfect Fit

"One Size Fits All" is
Just a fable,
There's no truth to it at all.
Your heart knows it,
Your eyes see it
In the mirror on the wall.

Look around you!
Friends and strangers
Come in every shape and size.
Each one special,
Each one worthy,
In their loving Maker's eyes.

Fight the urge to
Start a diet,
Starving body, heart and soul.
Seek instead
A healthy balance,
Self-acceptance as your goal.

Try some movement,
Add some color,
Paint your canvas bold and bright.
Make the most of
This, your body.
Bet you'll find it fits just right!

— Liz Curtis Higgs
June 1993

Resources

Catalogues for Larger Women . . .

JUST MY SIZE Catalog
P. O. Box 748
Rural Hall, NC 27908-0748

SILHOUETTES
340 Poplar Street
Hanover, PA 17333-0069

JUST RIGHT!
P.O. Box 1020
Beverly, MA 01915-0720

BROWNSTONE WOMAN
Brownstone Studio
685 Third Avenue
New York, NY 10017-4024

I. MAGNIN
P.O. Box 2096
Oakland, CA 94604

Magazines for Larger Women . . .

RADIANCE
P.O. Box 30246
Oakland, CA 94604

BIG BEAUTIFUL WOMAN
P.O. Box 16958
N. Hollywood, CA 91615

Organizations of Interest to Larger Women . . .

Association for the Health Enrichment of Large Persons
ATTN: Joe McVoy, Ph.D.
P. O. Box C
Radford, VA 24143

Largely Positive
ATTN: Carol Johnson
P.O. Box 17223
Glendale, WI 53217

National Association to Advance Fat Acceptance (NAAFA)
ATTN: Sally E. Smith, Executive Director
P.O. Box 188620
Sacramento, CA 95818

Other Books of Interest . . .

Never Too Thin: Why Women Are at War with Their Bodies,
Roberta Pollack Seid, Ph.D., Prentice Hall, 1989.

Bodylove, Rita Freedman, Harper & Row, 1988.

Great Shape: The First Exercise Guide for Large Women,
Pat Lyons and Debby Burgard, Bull Publishing, 1990.

Fat Is Not a Four-letter Word, Charles Roy Schroeder, Ph.D.,
Chronimed Publishing, 1992.

Making Peace with Food, Susan Kano, Harper & Row, 1989.

Breaking All the Rules, Nancy Roberts, Penguin Books,
1985.

Inner Eating, Shirley Billigmeier, Oliver-Nelson Books,
1991.

Big and Beautiful, Ruthanne Olds, Acropolis Books Ltd.,
1982.

Overcoming the Dieting Dilemma, Neva Coyle, Bethany
House, 1991.

Don't Diet, Dale Atrens, Ph.D., William Morrow & Company, 1988.

Rethinking Obesity, Paul Ernsberger and Paul Haskew, Human Sciences Press, 1987.

Overcoming Fear of Fat, Laura S. Brown and Esther D. Rothblum, Harrington Park Press, 1989.

The Obsession: Reflections on the Tyranny of Slenderness, Kim Chernin, Harper & Row, 1981.

The Dieter's Dilemma, William Bennett, M.D., and Joel Gurrin, Basic Books, 1982.

Never Satisfied, Hillel Schwartz, The Free Press, Macmillan, Inc., 1986.

The Hungry Self: Women, Eating and Identity, Kim Chernin, Harper & Row, 1985.

The Beauty Myth, Naomi Wolf, Anchor Books, 1992.

When Food Is Love, Geneen Roth, Penguin Books, 1992.

The Survey

Here are the questions we posed to the 200+ women featured in *"One Size Fits All" and Other Fables!*

1. Please circle your age range:
   18-24   25-34   35-44   45-54   55-64   65+

2. Please state your dress size:

3. How long have you been this size?

4. Is anyone in your family also your size? Who?

5. What words come to mind when you think of your body?

6. What comments do you receive about your size, and who says them?

7. What thoughts or experiences come to mind when you think of the word "DIET?"

8. If you are employed, what is your occupation?

   Does your size have any impact on your job? If so, please explain:

9. What are your favorite hobbies, social activities, etc.?

   Does your size have any impact on your social life?
   Please explain:

10. What are some of the challenges you face because of your size?

11. How might *"One Size Fits All" and Other Fables* be most helpful to you? What do you hope it will include?

12. Additional thoughts for *"One Size Fits All" and Other Fables* (personal discoveries, funny stories, memories, or your own "encouraging" words):

   Here's a Bonus Question: What are the 3 biggest "fables" about weight/size?

1. _____

2. _____

3. _____

Send to: Liz Curtis Higgs
          P. O. Box 43577
          Louisville, KY 40253-0577

Notes

Fable #1: "There's A Thin Person Trapped Inside You"

1. "Cher: Fit & Feisty at 46," *National Enquirer*, January 1983 Swimsuit Special, 51.
2. Roberta Pollack Seid, Ph.D., *Never Too Thin* (New York: Prentice Hall, 1989), 97.
3. "Plastic Surgery—for Under-Forties," *Self*, September 1989, 228.
4. Ibid.
5. Psalm 139:14.
6. Seid, *Never Too Thin*, 27.
7. Proverbs 7:4.

Fable #2: "All It Takes Is a Little Willpower"

1. "Growth and Recession in the Diet Industry, 1989-1996,"*Obesity and Health*, January/February 1992.
2. "Let Them Eat Cake," *Newsweek*, 17 August 1992, 57.
3. Seid, *Never Too Thin*, 105.
4. Ibid, 107.
5. Ibid, 138.
6. Nancy Roberts, *Breaking All the Rules* (New York: Viking Penguin, 1987), 34.
7. Susan Kano, *Making Peace with Food* (New York: Harper & Row, 1989), 3.
8. Sally Squires, "Which Diet Works," *Working Woman*, October 1992, 92.
9. Carol Johnson, "Fasting: The Problem Lies in the Fast Part," *On a Positive Note*, February 1990, 3.
10. Janice Kaplan, "Regardless of How Fit Women Are, We Still Want to be Thin," *Self*, September 1989, 195.

11. Adriane Fugh-Berman, M.D., *The National Women's Health Network News*, May/June 1992, 3.

Fable #3: "You're Just Big Boned"

1. Carol Johnson, "Fasting: The Problem Lies in the Fast Part," *On a Positive Note*, February 1990, 4.
2. "Medical Myths Debunked," *BBW*, April 1993, 44.
3. Ibid, 43.
4. "Special Edition," *Newsweek*, Winter/Spring 1990, 100.
5. Kim Chernin, *The Hungry Self* (New York: Harper & Row, 1985), 42.

Fable #4: "You Are What You Eat" (If That Were True, I'd Be Yogurt)

1. Seid, *Never Too Thin*, 4.
2. 1 Corinthians 6:12.
3. Mimi Sheraton, "Figures Can't Lie but . . . ," *Time*, 20 January 1986, 63.
4. David Garner, Ph.D., "Rent a New Thinner Body?" *Radiance*, Winter 1991, 42.
5. Shirley Billigmeier, *Inner Eating* (Nashville: Thomas Nelson, 1991), 162.
6. *The Random House Dictionary of the English Language* (New York: Random House, 1969), 562.
7. Kano, *Making Peace*, 203.

Fable #5: "All Fat People Are Lazy"

1. Pat Lyons and Debby Burgard, *Great Shape* (Palo Alto: Bull Publishing Company, 1990), 169.
2. Fugh-Berman, *The National Women's Health Network News*, 3.
3. Ibid.
4. Lyons and Burgard, *Great Shape*, 41.
5. Ann Diffily, "Weighty Matters," *Cross and Crescent*, Summer 1990, 33.
6. Kaplan, *Self*, 195.
7. Kano, *Making Peace with Food*, 55.

8. Pat Lyons, "Fat and Fit: An Idea Whose Time Has Come," *The National Women's Health Network News*, May/June 1992, 5.
9. Pat Lyons, "Improving the Health, Fitness and Body Image of Large Women," Presentation to the American Public Health Association Annual Meeting, 12 November 1991.
10. 1 Timothy 4:8.
11. Colossians 2:20–22.
12. Colossians 2:16.

Fable #6: "Things Would Be Perfect If I Were a Size 10"

1. Seid, *Never Too Thin*, 3.
2. Ibid, 15.
3. Dr. Esther Rothblum, "Weight and Social Stigma," *N.A.A.F.A. Newsletter*, November 1992, 6.

Fable #7: "Large Women Adore Wearing Double Knit" (It's So Flattering!)

1. Seid, *Never Too Thin*, 71.
2. Ibid, 81.
3. Ibid, 95.
4. 1 Peter 3:3–4.
5. Seid, *Never Too Thin*, 44.
6. Lois Anzelowitz, "You Call This Progress?" *Working Woman*, October 1992, 95.
7. Michael Cader, *Eat These Words* (New York: Harper Collins, 1991), 13.

Fable #8: "You'll Love Yourself More If You Lose Weight"

1. Josh McDowell, *His Image, My Image* (San Bernardino: Here's Life, 1984), 11.
2. Ardena Shankar, "Self-Esteem and Personal Responsibility," *N.A.A.F.A. Newsletter*, May/June 1992, 6.
3. Carole Shaw interviewed on the *Jenny Jones Show*, 8 April 1992.

4. "Some Folks Are Born To Yo-Yo," *People*, 13 January, 1992, 76.
5. Proverbs 23:20–21.
6. Matthew 11:19.
7. 1 Samuel 16:7.
8. Esther 2:12.
9. Garner, *Radiance*, 37.
10. Judy Simon, M.S., R.D., "Women's Struggle with Body Image," Presentation for the Mid-Michigan Regional Medical Center "Just Between Women" program, November 2, 1991.

Fable #9: "Big People Are Always Jolly" (Ha!)

1. Jane Thomas Noland, *Laugh It Off* (Minneapolis: CompCare, 1991), 4.
2. Sandy Summers Head, *Sizing Up* (New York: Simon and Schuster, 1989), 21.
3. Paul E. McGee, Ph.D., *Humor: Its Origin and Development* (San Francisco: W. H. Freeman, 1979), 206.
4. Ibid, 205.
5. Joel Goodman, "Smile! You're On, Allen Funt!" *Laughing Matters*, Volume 3, Number 1, 10.
6. Proverbs 17:22.

Fable #10: "You'll Never Get a Man"

1. Kaplan, *Self*, 195.

Fable #11: "You Can Lose It If You Really Want To"

1. Gina Kolata, "The Burdens of Being Overweight," *The New York Times*, 22 November 1992, 38.
2. Carole Shaw interviewed on the *Jenny Jones Show*, 8 April 1992.
3. Gina Kolata, *The New York Times*, 38.
4. Beverly Fortune, "Diet Centers: A User's Guide," *Lexington Herald-Leader*, 17 January 1993, J-1.
5. Ibid, J-2.

6. Carol Johnson, "I Thought You'd Tell Me How to Lose Weight and Keep It Off...," *On a Positive Note*, September 1992, 1.
7. Ibid.
8. Kaplan, *Self*, 194.
9. Charles Roy Schroeder, Ph.D., *Fat Is Not a Four-Letter Word* (Minneapolis: Chronimed Publishing, 1992), 140.
10. Rita Freedman, *Beauty Bound* (London: Columbus Books, 1988), 151.
11. Proverbs 4:18.
12. Freedman, *Beauty Bound*, 151.
13. Carol Johnson, "Research Review," *On a Positive Note*, March 1992, 6.
14. Carol Johnson, "Research Roundup," *On a Positive Note*, June 1992, 7.
15. Psalm 109:24.
16. Quoted by Pay Lyons in interview with author, January 1993.
17. Alicia Sandhei, "There is Change," *N.A.A.F.A. Newsletter*, June 1991, 3.

Fable #12: "One Size Fits All"

1. Erma Bombeck, *The Erma Bombeck 1992 Desk Calendar*, (Kansas City: Andrews and McMeel, a Universal Press Syndicate Company), 11 May, Monday.
2. Schroeder, *Fat is Not a Four-letter Word*, 28.
3. Ann Landers, "Society Gives Women Unreal View of Perfect Body Image," *Detroit Free Press*, 6 July 1992, 2D.
4. Schroeder, *Fat is Not a Four-letter Word*, 49.
5. Pat Lyons, "Fat and Fit," 5.
6. Schroeder, *Fat is Not a Four-letter Word*, 110.
7. Ibid, 298.

About the Author

A native of eastern Pennsylvania, Liz Curtis Higgs spent ten years traveling up and down the dial as a popular radio personality in five states. It was in the Bluegrass State of Kentucky that she discovered the thrill of speaking before a live audience: "An Encourager" ® was born.

Since becoming a professional speaker in 1987, Liz has presented hundreds of humorous, encouraging programs for businesses, associations, hospitals, and churches all over America. She is a member of the National Speakers Association, and earned their prestigious designation of C.S.P. — Certified Speaking Professional — in 1993.

As a member of the Fellowship of Merry Christians and the American Association for Therapeutic Humor, Liz believes in the value of laughter. She fills her presentations, her writing, and her life with a healthy dose of fun. She also enjoys singing in the choir, watching old movies, shopping for clothes and playing Go Fish with her family.

Liz received her Bachelor of Arts in English from Bellarmine College in 1990 — finally! She and her husband Bill, a computer systems specialist, have two young children, Matthew and Lillian, and one old house in the country, east of Louisville, Kentucky.